The Immortal's Handbook

A Compelling Guide
For Getting Out of Life _Alive_

by

Mikal Nyght

A Look at Life
From the Far Side of Death

Author: Mikal Nyght
Publisher: Eye Scry Publications

ISBN: 978-1-942415-37-4
Copyright © September, 2020
All rights reserved

WHOLESALE INFORMATION

For information about wholesale rates,
or to order additional copies, please email us at…

info@eyescrypublications.com

Visit the author's website at
www.immortalis-animus.com

Have a conversation with the author at:
www.immortalis-animus.com/forum/index.php

Dedication...

*For The One
who is
The All*

永

Eternity

**Life is the childhood
of our immortality.**

– Johann Wolfgang von Goethe

PREAMBLE RAMBLE

A Funny Thing Happened
On the way to The Way

This book isn't what it started out to be. What ever is? *Who* ever is? We evolve. We change. We go on magnificent quests. We occasionally discover that our quest-mates have wandered off into other dimensions of their own creation until eventually we find ourselves alone – and all of this is exactly as it should be.

Originally, this book was envisioned by a dear friend and long-time apprentice, and began with the tentative title, "*Questions To Advanced Beings.*" It was to be a series of questions gathered from seekers all over the world, accompanied by responses garnered via gnosis (silent knowing) from beings all over the multiverse.

While this started out quite well, my friend was mysteriously befallen by a series of health issues that derailed her for a considerable length of time, and in such a way that I began to consider the possibility – as I have many times – that those who fly too close to the truth often get their wings singed, or worse. Put another way, there are those "advanced beings" who *want* the human race to have this information so that they may break the chains of their imprisonment in the matrix; but there are far *more* forces (many right here on Planet Earth) that do *not* want information such as what is contained in these pages to ever fall into the hands of mere mortals.

While this obviously sounds quite sinister, it is also – sadly – quite true, as I'm sure more than a few seekers have discovered along the way to The Way. As a result, and what I consider to be an ongoing effort to prevent this information from coming to light, the decision was made for myself to take the more visible reins of the project, with my friend collaborating from a more discreet distance.

That being the case, *The Immortal's Handbook* became what we hope will be a comprehensive guide for getting out of life *alive*. In these pages you will find facts, fictions, and allegorical anecdotes alike. Not all were penned by myself, a few having been gleaned from gnosis prior to when I came on board the project. I mention this only because it should be noted by all seekers that truth is often relative to the truthsayer, and there is no such thing as "absolute truth" despite what some will try to tell you.

And yet, I will contradict myself by saying that the *only* absolute truth is that of unconditional love. Without it, there would be no reason to live forever. Love is the reason – the backbone of the immortal realm.

I will therefore caution you to read not only *this* book but *anything* that crosses your path with an open mind and also with a discriminating third eye. While some of the truths and anecdotes in these pages might rattle your rancor, that's to be expected when confronting anything that threatens your status quo – which is precisely what this book is intended to do. What concerns me more is that seekers practice silent knowing with a state of the art bullshit detector securely installed in their personal mainframe.

You will find things here that resonate deeply with you, and others that don't. Pay attention – but in the final analysis, make sure you are paying attention to your higher self (your Other/twin/double) and not just the terrified tremblings of the internal dialog, who would much prefer that you go to church on Sunday and read only your Bible and whatever approved textbooks are recommended at school (so long as they don't promote evolution or thinking for yourself).

Find your truth. Know yourself. Live forever.

Some days entire centuries pass
while I gather the gnosis of candles
beyond the illusion of time.

INTRODUCTION

Even the stars
are only momentary companions
to those such as us.
Sure this is what you want?

————

Immortality is nothing to be trifled with. It isn't some transient phase one goes through as a result of teen angst or midlife crisis or the aches and pains of old age. Those who choose to pursue the immortal condition would hopefully do so with the foreknowledge that it is forever.

For.

Ever.

Most mortals cannot even begin to wrap their minds around the depth of the word itself, thinking instead in limited increments of time. How casually the word is bandied about. "I will love you forever." "Nothing lasts forever." "Forever and a day isn't nearly long enough."

Perhaps a more pertinent perspective would be in the soul-deep cry of Freddie Mercury. *"Who wants to live forever?"*

In reality, *forever* is the milieu in which the fledgling infant known as Time takes his first awkward steps, only to get bored with it all and eventually fall aside. And that is when the window of opportunity opens, allowing brief glimpses into what writers have alternately called 'the end of time' or 'the land beyond time' or 'the land time forgot.'

This is the milieu of Shadowland – the blank slate upon which seekers and immortals alike create their own individual world which is entirely subjective and, paradoxically, entirely available to those whom the seeker might invite for a tour, a vacation, or a shared eternity. It's interesting to note that this concept has probably always existed, answering to various names throughout history. Perhaps the most famous might be 'Through the Looking Glass' or 'Over the Rainbow.'

Does this imply that Shadowland is merely a fantasy, a fitful and fanciful dream? Not in the least. And quite the contrary. Dreams and fantasies are the building blocks of all realities.

From a quantum perspective, anything you can imagine already exists, and so Dorothy *created* Oz when she longed for it, when she sang it into being, when she Dreamed it alive. A popular statement, often repeated in my own works is simply this: *"All things exist within the realm of possibility, but only some things will be forced to go through the motions of actually occurring."*

To take that one step further, the seeker needs to internalize the idea that the ability to create and inhabit

Shadowland is every bit as much a part of the natural human inventory as breathing or learning to walk. Unfortunately, it is a piece of the puzzle that has been whittled away and denounced by religions and governments for centuries, until now it is most often viewed as an aberration requiring extensive therapy in a medical facility somewhere on the outskirts of what is commonly accepted as sanity.

Why might this be so? Brutally put, those in positions of power want to *keep* that power for themselves and have no regard for you, me, or anyone else. The moment a seeker realizes they really *are* the most powerful being in the universe, religions and governments and the new world order fall face down in the mud, impotent clowns, no longer needed and – more importantly – no longer *tolerated* as the icons of mental, intellectual, and spiritual slavery they have set themselves up to be.

If Shadowland is the self-generated milieu of the immortals, *forever* is the infinite and, at times, unbearable silence between the tick and the tock of the quantum clock. It is the immeasurable expanse in *between* the increments of time itself, and as such it can neither be calculated nor captured. Even by the immortals, it can barely be understood except through the experience of it – which is not at all linear and at times not even altogether cohesive from a singular point of view.

[[What the hell does that mean, Mikal?]]

It means that what many traditionally think of as past lives are actually manifestations of the immortal Other moving through space and time in a random but altogether controlled manner designed to provide the mortal seeker with Knowledge not otherwise available to a being who is trapped inside an organic meat suit within the hungry belly of deadly time.

In this way – this ability of the Other to transcend time and space – forever is the milieu of true immortality. It is not some transitory physical longevity that can be ended with a wooden stake to the heart or a silver bullet or a rampaging Peterbilt or even the ravages of old age and disease. Instead, it is a continuity of awareness and cohesion that extends in all directions and into every unmapped cranny of space and time, including the realms of the past and the future of not only the big blue marble known as Earth, but into the history and future history of every world and every square centimeter of dark matter and dark energy ever to be conceived or perceived.

And that is only the beginning of the beginning of forever, the tiny seed containing the entirety of eternity.

If you can wrap your mind around what that might actually mean, and if you find the concept desirable as a reality and not just some fleeting fantasy, you might have the barest beginnings of what it will take to get out of your mortal life alive.

Perhaps one of the hardest tasks a seeker faces is learning to let go of what you might *think* are reasonable and perhaps even scientific "facts." Virtually everything you *believe* about the world and about yourself is the result of corrupted data. Like the old game of "telephone" – wherein one person whispers a comment to the person on her left, and this continues until at least 10 people have been given the phrase and asked to repeat it. By the time it comes full circle, it will almost never be in alignment with the original statement posed at the beginning.

Real life is no different. Your parents told you something they learned from *their* parents, who in turn had learned it from your great grandparents, and on back in the crannies of time until, by the time it reaches *you* it has become little more than a twisted and warped version of whatever archaic truth *might* once have existed.

Letting go of what you believe is difficult because chances are you don't even realize you believe something until it is challenged. Do you believe in ghosts? (Probably not – that's absurd, right?) Do you believe in vampires? (Of course not – just the ramblings of sexually frustrated housewives, yes?) Do you believe in immortality? (Don't be silly, Mikal. All things die.)

Do they? Who said so, and why do you automatically believe it? Have you personally scoured every corner of the Earth? Can you say with certainty that the stranger sitting next to you on the bus *isn't* a ghost or a vampire or an immortal of some description?

In these pages, I will talk about disembodied spirits, vampires, aliens, and tulpas – because, contrary to popular belief, metaphysical entities don't need your permission to exist. Whether you believe in them or not makes very little difference... *unless* your insistence on clinging to those beliefs is what's preventing *you* from seeing the door to your own evolution.

Before you can even consider immortality as a viable possibility, you have to let go of all the things that insist on telling you it's impossible – whether in your mother's voice, the droning sermons of your priest, or your favorite physics teacher from high school.

The only thing standing between you and your chance at forever is yourself. Or more accurately, it is the programs you have been outfitted with since the first human prototype crawled out of the primordial sludge and reared up on its hind legs, or since the first beta version of some inconceivable computer simulation was launched by a kid in a science class on Rigel Prime. (But more on that when we tackle the troubling notion, *"Are We A Computer Simulation?"*) If we are, then it's also conceivable that time and space are only pixels on that kid's iPhone, but even if that *is* the case, the primary goal for those who choose it is the same as if we are the descendents of Zugg and Ling-Lang, First Man and First Woman.

The goal is to become *more* than the transient organic matter that comprises the meat suit. The goal is

11

getting out of the matrix intact – whether transferring awareness from the organic form to the inorganic Other; or if we *are* a computer simulation, the task of evolving our rudimentary awareness sufficiently so that it can escape the matrix in which it is housed and have a modicum of a chance to survive and thrive in whatever "the real world" might turn out to be.

In the bigger version of the big picture, it really doesn't matter if humans are *in* the matrix, or if the matrix has spun them into being as units of awareness in some experiment on some far distant planet in the Klaatu Nebula. What does matter is that you are a unique unit of consciousness.

> **You are the only one of your kind. There has never been another one like you and never will be, because your experiences have shaped your memories, and your memories have generated an individuated identity, and somewhere in that equation, you either want to survive with that identity intact... or you don't. You either want to be *I-Am* or you will choose by default to be nothing at all.**

And guess what? It's okay if you don't want to take upon yourself the difficult and perhaps seemingly impossible task of becoming greater than the sum of your mortal parts. It isn't for everybody, as most who *do* decide to give it a go eventually discover. Most who start along the way turn back and run screaming for their familiar comfort zones more than once. Some stay there, safe in their place in the sun, while others gradually creep up on the prospect of immortality like stalking some elusive and infinitely dangerous beast.

In so many ways, the desire for it has to border on a compulsion, even what some would say is an obsession and an addiction to awareness itself. Those who feel such a state of being aren't content to think in terms of reincarnation, for the downside to that is that it appears that there really isn't a *continuity* of consciousness, no sense of identity that comes into a new biological form with *your* memories intact and available to use as a handy database for navigating your "next life."

From an immortal perspective – or even from the perspective of a gifted human seer – reincarnation is one more illusion spoon-fed to the masses to keep them complacent, imbued with a hope that is really nothing more than wishful thinking. What good does it do to pass through life and death only to be reborn as a homeless beggar on the streets of Bangkok or even the heir to a fortune amassed by some drug lord in the jungles of Colombia? If you aren't *you*, then *you* haven't really survived at all. Instead, your atoms have been redistributed, but any sense of personal identity is lost in the silent black whirlwind that is the domain of Death itself.

But instead of talking about what you stand to lose, let's talk for a moment about what you might gain by attaining the immortal condition. First, let's just state for the record that true immortality consists of inhabiting what is commonly thought of as an energy body. Now don't throw the book over your shoulder and run back to your favorite religion, but take a moment to consider that *all* things are energy at their core. Yes, even *you.*

Right now, mortal or immortal, you are made of energy that is eternal – it's always been here and always will be. It cannot be created or destroyed, but can only change form (for those who were diddling their cell phones in first semester physics and failed to internalize that very fundamental statement).

The difference is that when you are in a mortal body, you are susceptible to whatever dangers exist that could extinguish that fragile existence. Stepping into the Other (the energy body, the higher self, the astral body, the dreaming body) doesn't mean becoming some invisible woo-woo haunting the nearest Buddhist temple and frightening the local monks. Instead, it means shedding the organic cocoon in order to embrace the evolving butterfly. Common old analogy, but nonetheless applicable.

What do you stand to gain by grasping your immortality? Only everything. Most of all, you gain the *opportunity* to go on existing – not always in the same way you've come to think of as human life, but nonetheless *Be-ing* in ways that are profoundly enhanced and expanded when compared to traditional, organic human life.

This brings up the inevitable question and impending argument against immortality wherein someone in the back row pipes up with, "But immortality would be boring as hell, Mikal! I can barely get through the tedious routines of my human life. Get up in the morning, take a leak, brush hair and teeth, shower, get dressed, go to work, pretend to care what everybody did over the weekend, eat, sleep, shit, rinse and repeat. If I thought I had to do that for the next thousand years, I'd cut off my own head with a butter knife!"

Note to the hecklers: eternity isn't linear and immortals don't adhere to routines unless it is simply their predilection to do so out of habit – a habit that quickly diminishes as the newbie settles in to the realities of their profoundly altered awareness and enhanced abilities. The holographic universe is somewhat like a gigantic minuscule round rectangular box containing all of "time" – past history and future history and all the infinite possibilities that lie between the mysterious quanta of time itself. In between every nano-second are trillions of units of immeasurable space-time, and in between those quanta are more of the same – each unit absolutely infinite in all directions.

14

What this really boils down to is that most immortals and even many advanced practitioners have the ability to experience non-linear time by stepping outside the tedious progression of one day into the next. By moving one's reference point, one is able to localize (manifest awareness) within any point on the space-time continuum, or in the in-between of all those spaces existing at right angles to time itself.

In addition to throwing off the noose of time, perhaps one of the most important things you gain is the ability to live without the constant fear and pressure of Death itself. Whether you realize it or not, while in human form, there is a relentless if subliminal awareness that time is running out. Every breath you take is one breath closer to the end. *Tick tock tick tock.*

By the time you turn 45, chances are you are closer to the end than the beginning, and while that might serve as motivation to pick up the pace and do all those things on your bucket list, the downside is that you're already beginning to lose a certain amount of physical stamina and mental ambition. Sure, there are exceptions. Maybe you're one of them. Still fit as a Stradivarius and in perfect tune with the world at large. Maybe you even ran a marathon last year. Good for you. (*How's that bum knee? Did you tell anyone about the chest pains you had around mile 15?*)

And what happens around the time you turn 50? 60? Still think you can get your degree in medicine and find the cure for cancer? Still think you can climb K-2? Still think your wife hasn't noticed those little blue pills hidden in your sock drawer for those sadly dull and routine Thursday nights?

Face it. Mortality is invariably fatal – and in ways that not only cause the physical body to deteriorate, but the mental and intellectual prowess as well. Not only are you staring down the leaky barrel of adult diapers, but after the third time you walk into a room and don't remember why, you wander off to sit on the porch with the cat, whose name you also can't recall.

Obviously immortality takes care of all that jazz – zips it up in a convenient body bag and ships it off to an old bone yard known as The Past.

I was recently asked what happens to the seeker who attains all manner of wisdom and enlightenment during their lifetime, only to lose it to dementia in old age. Stated as simply as possible, once something is gained it can never be lost because that is the nature of the holographic universe. Become a full-fledged wizard today, get struck by lightning tomorrow and lose all brain function, you will *still* be a full-fledged wizard when you transcend your mortal life and step into the energetic structure that is the Other.

Just words, of course, lost in translation, but a concept that gradually becomes clear to those who pursue the path for any length of time. Even if your physical body doesn't remember who or even what it is, everything you have ever experienced is stored within the Other. If you've done the work, your Other will know what to do when the time comes.

Immortality is a passport to possibility and opportunity. Instead of being confined to a limited span of time, the seeker who steps into the Other now has the real chance to actually *do* all those things the mortal self could only dream about. Live a lifetime or two as a doctor if that kind of thing appeals to you. Live another lifetime as a lawyer if you enjoy being hated. Be a poet or a politician or simply an independent unit of awareness with no particular form at all. There are no time limits and no term limits.

And so another word for immortality is freedom. Freedom from fear. Freedom from death. Freedom from time itself.

But this brings us to the crux of the matter. *How* to actually attain the immortal condition.

Though I don't normally include exercises in my teachings, you might find a few scattered throughout these pages, hopefully disguised as common sense.

The first and most important would involve a daily meditation on one thing. Ask yourself this: *What do I believe and how did I come to believe it?* Followed immediately by: *And why do I believe that _what_ I believe is actually true?*

When you strip away all the layers of accumulated bullshit, you'll see that the answer is always the same. For as long as you *believe* something is impossible, it will always *remain* impossible.

Get out of your own way.

– Mikal Nyght, July 2020

*In Shadowland
the four cardinal directions are
Time, Night, Antimatter and Singularity.*

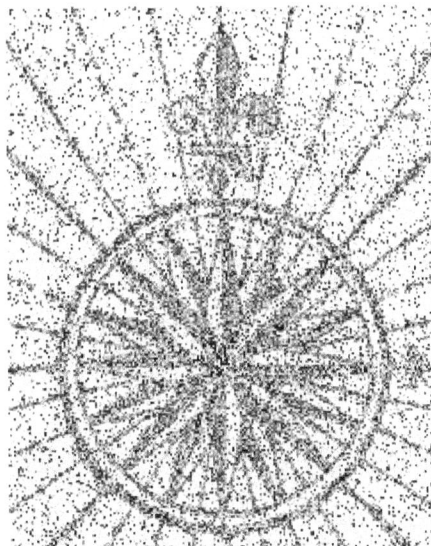

I will not always speak in a straightforward manner, because you have been conditioned to hear the words but not the intent behind them. So at times I will whisper a mist of poetry underneath the doorway of your mind, into your heart, where – if we are favored by Fate – it may lodge like a seedling, nurtured into being with a dangerous promise of something larger than the world as you think you know it; a tiny kernel that might lie dormant for years, then finally grow into a tree of infinite knowledge – with branches star-fed and leaves of forbidden wisdom that has always been with you, waiting for your gnosis to unfold.

PART ONE
Through the Looking Glass

*"Now, here, you see, it takes all the running
you can do, to keep in the same place. If you want
to get somewhere else, you must run at least
twice as fast as that."*
— Lewis Carroll

———

Identifying Our Identity

*How would you define yourself? Who are you? <u>What
are you?</u>*

While it is impossible to truly define any sovereign
being, I would say simply that *I-Am.* That is not an
evasive answer, but an honest one, and the only one
that genuinely addresses the question of identity –
whether mine, yours, or anyone else's. I have answered
to a thousand names in as many lifetimes, all of which
are a *single* lifetime when viewed from a cohesive, non-
linear perspective of totality[1].

There is only one world, divided infinitely by perception.

By human definition, it could be said that I am an
immortal in a quantum state, though even that is a
misleading label – and immortals eschew labels in the
same manner your Superman would eschew kryptonite.

---

[1] **Totality of Oneself**: The state of being that exists when mortal human and
immortal Other conjoin. This would encompass the mortal's full scope of memory,
in addition to the Other's vast knowledge amassed during the course of thousands
of parallel lives.

Labels are limitations. To call oneself an immortal is to create an idea in the mind of others, and in doing so, both the speaker and the listener become enslaved by the definitions that seek to clarify but ultimately only obfuscate.

For that reason, it is best to think of me and others like myself in terms of how they *feel* to you, how you perceive them, and simply call them by a name they have given you or a name you give to them. Once upon a very long time ago, I had a cat whom I called Claudius. In all likelihood, it wasn't really his name, but that is how he *felt* to me and so it is how I knew him even though *he* probably considered the name absurd. But he answered to it because it meant food and attention and a warm place to sleep in a world that had not yet come to appreciate feline companionship.

Who am I?

This is perhaps the most important question you will ever ask – not of me, but of yourselves. What you will discover is that there is no single, definitive answer that will satisfy your family, your friends, or even your perception of yourself from one day to the next. Such is the nature of the search, for in asking the question, you begin to explore the possible answers – not as intellectual gibberish, but as experiences linked together through the strange and mutable faculty of memory.

In that way, I could tell you that *I-Am* the scent of the sea near Piraeus on an October evening when the rains come to stir the essential elements common to any port city. The groaning creak of wood from vessels lolling lazily in their berths at night. The scent of cooking wafting out through open windows. The soft murmur of conversations between lovers, the staccato bursts between rivals arguing over meaningless stances. Crunch of sand beneath my boots, different here than in all the world, for no reason other than this is Greece when most still believed in the old gods, when time was a slipknot of blurred seasons instead of the master of one's fate.

I am that.

And *I-Am* the accumulation of all else I have experienced – as are all beings. You are the memory of being comforted in your mother's arms as an infant. The cold nuzzle of a beloved dog's nose seeking attention in the dark. The first shy kiss of your first true love. The horrific experience of losing a loved one to the fatal embrace of Death. Forgotten wildflowers blooming in the cracks of a sidewalk. Moonglow on a still and tepid lake in the dead heat of summer. A songbird in the distance, linked to some long-past memory lost in time.

As to *what* I am, that is perhaps an interesting story for those who like tales that are seated in truth, but regarded as fanciful fictions by most who would consider themselves sane and rational members of the consensus reality.

> **The consensus as it presently exists is essentially the asylum turned wrong-side-out, with the mentally diseased running the factory in the same way old proverbs speak of foxes providing security for the hen house.**

Never in the history of your civilization has the world been so divided, but even that – the age-old chaos of politics and religion – is meaningless folly in the end of the beginning. I say "in the end of the beginning" because seekers inevitably come to a crossroads where it is altogether necessary to put aside their existing beliefs in order to embrace a new beginning rooted entirely in direct personal experience. And because it is not possible during a mortal human lifetime to experience *everything* directly, you are faced with the task of determining what experiences and knowledge might matter to you, and what would only be more indulgence in more fatal folly.

Do you want or need to visit the pyramids in Egypt as an adjunct to your personal journey, or are you willing to accept on the word of others that the pyramids even exist, and are seemingly the source of great mystery and power? There is no right or wrong answer. There is only what matters to *you*, considered in tandem with the treacherous stalker known to most by the 4-letter word, Time. How much time do you have, and how will you use it to your best advantage?

If you want to know who *I-Am*, I will tell you a story that begins with the words "Once upon a long, long time ago in a land far away..."

Though I was once human, comprised of mortal flesh and blood, that ceased to be the case when I met a man who was destined to become my teacher, my liberator, my beloved, and my most-despised tyrant. Teacher and liberator in the sense that it was he who was responsible for lifting the veil of false beliefs and cultural lies from my eyes; beloved and despised because I could not help but love him for the clarity and freedom he bestowed on me. Yet at the same time I hated him for robbing me of what I had previously hoped to accomplish: a happy life with a wife, children, friends, and the simplicity of farming the vineyard that had been in my family for as long as anyone could recall.

I should point out that I am not speaking metaphorically when I say that my mentor changed me entirely. I do not mean a mere altering of my perception or the manner in which I had previously experienced the world. I became changed down to a quantum level. What was previously flesh and bone became instead a construct of pure energy – which, ironically, is precisely what all things *are* at their inorganic core, but which becomes trapped in an organic matrix somewhere around the so-called "age of reason" due to the ingrained beliefs of the consensus at large.

Humans are ultimately a chrysalis in the process of unfurling, but all too often they become ensnared in the cocoon to such an extent that they lose the ability to emerge, spread their wings, and fly free.

> **What should logically already *be* immortal becomes mortal through the belief in and experience of the anomaly known as Death, and over a long period of time it becomes the core nature of the human organism to actually *be* organic instead of the inorganic energy it truly *is* beyond all words, language, and programming to the contrary.**

I refer to Death as an anomaly because it is an aberration in the matrix itself – a design flaw if you will – a quasi-intelligent virus that has invaded and mutated the genetic and psychological programming of Man as a species. This is one primary reason that legends of immortality exist in the ancient literatures as far back as recorded history goes.

Before Man was mortal, he was *immortal*, but once the virus was introduced into the equation, it became a contagion that rapidly spread like no other pandemic ever has or ever will, and resulted not only in altering the genetic make-up of the human race, but – far more importantly – in altering the manner in which humans think, live, and ultimately die.

Who or what introduced Death into the mix? No way to truly know, and speculation is little more than mental masturbation reserved for high-brow academics and teenagers emerging into the budding awareness that they really *aren't* omniscient despite what they tend to believe.

However it came into being, Death is here now and must be acknowledged and confronted as the most contemptible and morally bankrupt enemy ever to sneak in through the crack between the worlds. Myths and legends are abundant, of course. Eve was an apple-toting temptress seduced by a snake. Coyote got outvoted by a bunch of arrogant birds and Death was favored over Sleep. Hades got gobbled up by Night, and Death followed in the aftermath forevermore. Take your pick.

But it was the very existence of Death that motivated my mentor (I'll call him Marcus for no particular reason) to create within me the fundamental alterations that would result in eliminating the genetic coding to which Death had attached itself. Put simply, he didn't *give* me immortality. He *removed* Death *from* me by fundamentally rewriting both the organic edifice and – far more importantly – the psychological pathways that govern the manner in which the coding that makes us human is structured.

In very simple terms, he changed me from man to myth, from organic to inorganic, from mortal to immortal. I've been asked over the years if there was a single moment when *It* happened. Was there a flash of enlightenment when I merely stepped out of the lie and into the light?

Was there a ritual?

Of *course* there was a ritual. There is *always* a ritual – not because it is required by nature or any imaginary deity, but because it is what the human animal has been taught to believe leads to that transformational moment. And unless that belief can be assuaged or eliminated altogether (the latter of which is virtually impossible through normal channels), the ritual serves as a binding force between What-Is-Believed and What-Becomes-Known.

As an example, for those of the Christian faith, the ritual is that moment of surrender to their God through the ceremony of baptism – the subject goes down into the symbolic waters of Death and is reborn in God's image, washed clean of all sins, immortal forever and ever, amen. At least that's how the legends go, though I have yet to met any *real* immortals who gained their immortality through the baptismal pond. But no matter.

While I could describe the ritual itself, it would be extraneous, except to say that by the time Marcus enacted it, he knew me well enough to know it was one of the prevailing myths of the culture in which I had been raised, and therefore because I had been exposed to it at an early age and had come to believe it wholly, it was the "right" ritual for *me*. Had the same ritual been enacted with another individual who had no belief in it, the transformation undoubtedly would not have worked. Therefore, it can be said that I am the end product of my beliefs – which were strong enough to carry me through the ritual itself and deliver me on the other side of it into what the ritual had always claimed would be the outcome.

> **A belief which was a lie became the truth – not because it *was* independently true, but because it was *made* true through the ironic belief in the lie.**

Paradoxes notwithstanding, Marcus made me an immortal because I *believed* he could. Irony at its finest.

In reality, of course, he did no such thing, but understood *my* disposition sufficiently to give me the power to *become* what I had always been: an inorganic being of energy, a being of light, an eternal structure in a finite and sadly mortal world.

If I Were King
A Look at Agendas

It's been said that everyone has an agenda. Do you?

It's interesting to note that most beings don't have an agenda at all, because until they are awakened, they are incapable of exerting the forces of Intent and the mystery of Will. Someone once asked what I would do if I were king of the world. My response? "I'd return the crown and run for the hills." After all, who would *really* want such a tedious obligation?

"If I, if I, were King!"
The Wizard of Oz

If I have an agenda at all, it is only to provide information to seekers, which they can choose to convert to knowledge-through-experience, or not. *Why bother?* some might ask.

Eternity is a large expanse of real estate, and might run the risk of becoming a lonely affair if there were not others with whom to share it. It's occasionally possible to share it with mortals, but that is both fleeting and infinitely sad – friends quickly come and go, like moths at the candle flame for such a brief while, beautiful but transient flickers of light.

For that reason, there is a powerful motivation to nurture those rare few individuals who can hold up their side of a conversation and who aren't afraid of the dark – that which exists in the night, and that which is their own sentient shadow. These are rare gems, raw and uncut, diamonds in the rough to an immortal's gaze.

Other beings might have different agendas – some rooted in altruism, some rooted in power, some spawned by grief or love or even fear. Yes, even an evolved being can experience fear – though not in the same way humans would experience it. For an immortal, fears are often based on the long calendar, for though we might survive even the destruction of the planet itself, the people and things we love would not. If a comet struck the Earth, an immortal could instantly will himself to be elsewhere – another world, another dimension, or another point in Time.

For these reasons and others, some of us seek to educate select humans in their bid for evolution. Additionally, there is a shared sense among many evolved beings that there is a responsibility to the Knowledge itself. This has been heavily debated, with no resolution ever attained or forthcoming – because who or what would judge whether such a responsibility exists? Or is it only an altruistic manifestation of self-importance on the part of the teacher, or perhaps a vain attempt to teach that which cannot be taught at all, but must be gleaned through the seeker's own relentless hunger for Life itself, in all its infinite manifestations?

Of Maps and Star Charts
Where the Beginning Began

What is your origin? Where do you come from?

As previously indicated, I was once human. But I am only One. There are many, and not all were *ever* human. Some are what you would call aliens or visitors.

Where do *they* come from? Most are from the star system known to you as Epsilon Eridani. Perhaps it isn't surprising, therefore, that there are countless works of fiction speculating about this region of space – as if the authors might subconsciously sense the origins of the aliens they portray in their fantastical tales.

Some have even speculated that the mythical planet Vulcan is located in the Epsilon Eridani system, and that there is more truth to *Star Trek* than most would dare to imagine. Whether that is true, time will tell perhaps, or perhaps the reader should decide for herself if some fictions are facts cleverly disguised as fictions.

After all, the immortals have been engaging in such practices since Time worm-holed its way into the mix, and there is more truth in your current fictions than you might realize – not to deceive or confuse you, but to prepare you for the awakening that is inevitable when the blinders of the consensus are removed from your third eye.

What is real is what you can perceive.

What you can perceive is governed largely by what you believe. Remove the restrictions of self-limiting beliefs, and what was impossible moments ago flowers into full bloom – partially as a result of your unfettered Will, but also because it has been there all along and you have, at last, given yourself permission to see[2] it.

---

[2] **To "see"** is the act of viewing the world (or anything within the world) according to its true nature, without the illusions and expectations we place onto the world through human programs. Seeing is the seeker's greatest asset and tool in being able to recognize the illusory nature of the consensual reality.

The other region from which some immortals come is known as The Betelgeuse Cluster. It is speculated that the visitors from this region might have an agenda that has very little to do with humans and could even be considered sinister by some. The primary star of the system, Betelgeuse, is believed to be near the end of its lifespan, possibly approaching supernova within the foreseeable event horizon – still thousands of years in the future, but nonetheless too close for comfort to a long-lived but now-endangered species.

The inhabitants of the system – many of whom are natural immortals[3] – will be forced to seek other worlds to inhabit. Some have speculated that Earth is being considered for the future home of the Betelgeusians, though that seems unlikely for a variety of reasons. More plausible, those who are visiting here are doing so as individuals with individual agendas rather than as advance scouts for any sort of mass landing.

What would the agenda be of these individuals? Most likely just to exist in peace. They are remarkably similar to humans in many ways, with the primary difference being that their bodies do not age beyond your Earth equivalent of 30, nor are they susceptible to disease.

It is commonly believed that the Betelgeusians may have been the race that originally seeded Earth, in particular the continent once known as Atlantis. All speculation, of course, but interesting as a topic of conversation around the fading glow of a red giant.

What can you tell us about Atlantis? Did ancient civilizations on this planet have technology like ours before they reached their end?

---

[3] **Natural immortals**: (also known as organic immortals) are those who were born as immortals, as opposed to someone who was transformed or attained the immortal condition through transmogrification or transcendence.

Those few immortals who claim to have witnessed the events say the end of Atlantis was a two-fold happening. Their technology was sufficiently advanced that it would make the gizmology of today pale by comparison. Their medical knowledge was unsurpassed and resulted in the average mortal lifespan eventually being 300 years or more. Though the exact timeline of these events is so ancient as to defy even racial memory, it is generally believed that the original starseeds were immortal, but eventually began breeding with a growing population of native humans, and for reasons not known to us now, the Death gene proved dominant in the offspring.

On the other side of the coin, technology had evolved at a rate much faster than spiritual/social/cultural awareness, especially with regard to the schism between the native humans and the starseeds. When a civil war inevitably broke out, the weapons were sufficient to create a vibrational anomaly of epic proportions – an event that catastrophically disrupted the electromagnetic and gravitational fields of the entire planet.

I am not a scientist and my explanations might not satisfy someone with greater techno-Knowing than I possess. However, what occurred was a magnetic storm resulting in a polar shift, or so the legends say. In all honesty, I wasn't there, for this was long before even my time.

Atlantis didn't sink as might happen eventually to Venice. Instead, it was instantly subsumed by a wave of such magnitude that all life was immediately obliterated, and the continent itself – the part that didn't break up – is now underneath a massive ice shelf near Antarctica. Again, this is the stuff of legends, but the immortals who profess to have direct knowledge of these events maintain that the location was very near the southern tip of Argentina and Chile, in between those two countries and the continent of Antarctica.

Others claim it was part of a land bridge connecting Antarctica to Northern Australia, and that New Zealand might well be parts of the Atlantean island-continent that broke away during the cataclysmic event. Obviously there is no way to discern the veracity of either claim, since immortals are notoriously direction-impaired as well as being consummate liars. Present company excepted, of course.

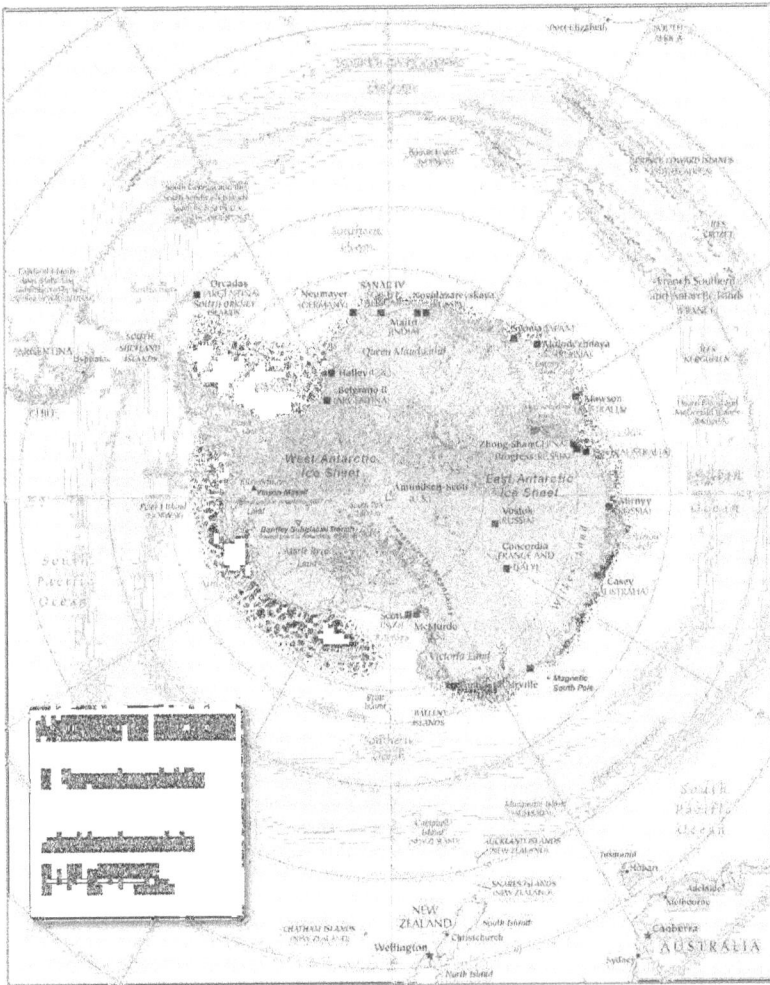

It is rumored that a few prescient individuals escaped the continent prior to the collapse, but because of the global scope of the event, whatever became of them is unknown.

Is *any* of it truly true? Who's to say? Rumors, legends, stories told in the fleeting aftermath of it all. The lesson is obvious, though it is equally obvious that history repeats itself because most lessons go unheeded. Sadly, the human species appears to be living in such a situation at the moment. Without immediate and profound change, the planet herself might survive, but most if not all organic life will be eliminated in a flash flood that would make Noah's debacle seem like a little drizzle by comparison. Some say it's already too late. I prefer to be slightly more optimistic, though with the current global situation being what it is, that optimism is rapidly turning into something else entirely.

We're going to need a bigger ark.

———

*We are not visitors
on this Earth
but landlords of space and time.*

PART TWO
The Mortal Realm

To attain the immortal condition
you must first survive the mortal world

*"You can do what serves your ego
or you can do what serves your agenda.
The choice is yours. 100%."*

———

What Do You Want?

Seems like a simple and straightforward question, but answering it might not prove to be quite so simple or straightforward at all. And until you know *what* you want, you will have little to no chance of attaining it.

This is where your intent as well as your abilities are put to the test. Feel the desire and define it, for it is the energy of the ache/hurt/want/need that will stir the particles of reality soup and bring forth your wishes into manifestation – not through wishing alone but through the actions that follow in the wake of the wish itself.

Ask yourself if the thing you desire most is a thing of the immortal realm or of the dayshine world. There are no wrong answers, except to lie to yourself. What you will discover if you are persistent is that love really *is* the reason. If you don't have sufficient passion and desire for something, it will remain nebulous as a passing ghost – real in one dimension but untouchable in another.

What do you *want?*

When you have the answer to that question – even if only a seemingly unreachable desire, it is the desire itself that generates the energy that puts the universal forces in motion. Once that energy is activated, all things become possible.

However, you must never forget: the needful desire is only the first step. Then comes the question – what will you *do* to manifest your desire? If you are seeking healing, what steps are you willing to take to improve your health? If you are seeking financial success in the dayshine world, are you willing to get a job or invent a better mousetrap or whatever it takes to *manifest* that desire? If you are seeking love among the ruins of this faltering world, how will you make yourself the object of someone else's ache/hurt/want/need?

Bluntly: how will you *be* the thing you seek? How will you become well, or at least better today than yesterday? How will you embody the concept of success? How will you be lovable in order to be loved? Are you looking outside the box or still trapped inside it?

Energy recognizes no boundaries or limitations.

The only way to fail is to quit.

What do *you* want?

Everything Begins With a Thought
Every Thought Begins a New Reality

The greatest challenge humans face on the road to immortality or even so-called "enlightenment" is the fact that they *are* human, and therefore prone to human frailties, not the least of which is the underlying acceptance of mortality as the natural and therefore acceptable state of human existence.

Nothing could be further from the truth.

I've said it before. At the risk of being called an old nag, I'll say it again: *You are the most powerful being in the universe.* You are comprised of stardust and moonbeams and fairy wings and everything in between, and all the magical things that have ever existed anywhere, and anything that can be imagined. Your component atoms have been here since before the Big Bang ejaculated, and will be here until the universe folds in on itself like an origami unicorn.

Everything begins with a thought. *[[There Mikal goes repeating himself again... old nag.]]* From a quantum perspective, anything you can imagine already exists – the thought itself calling it into existence, even if only as a self-fulfilling thoughtform. Ironic how these things work – perhaps more evidence that it's all a gigantic simulation operating under some sort of covert and incomprehensible rules, or perhaps an indication that we *are* the universe and therefore the universe cannot help but be imbued with magic and mysticism.

Some seekers think the quickest route to immortality is automatically the best route, but that isn't at all the case. Before you can even begin to perceive the immortal realm, you must first navigate the maze which is the dayshine world[4], the consensual reality, the machine, the matrix, the agreement.

Whatever you care to call it, *that* is where the journey begins, and too often it is where the journey ends. Why? Because the maze is filled with dead ends, false starts, questions that have no answers, and all those dangerous beliefs that keep you chained to all those responsibilities and obligations you've set up for yourself on what you've been told is The Road to Worldly Success.

The harsh reality is that worldly success doesn't even exist. In fact, it's one of the most compelling but dangerous illusions of all. *[[What? That's horseshit! I'm a plastic surgeon! I make more money in a day than Mikal would make in a century! *pounds chest like a proud monkey* I have 4 houses, a private jet, a trophy wife and*

---

[4] **Dayshine world**: The world of ordinary awareness, everyday life. The play. The matrix. It should be understood that most seekers have a dayshine life of one type or another. Meaning: humans all depend at some level on the real world until they evolve. Dayshine lives would include job, family, friends, everything that is of the world of matter and men.

3 mistresses! Mikal's just jealous 'cuz he didn't get a blow job this morning!]]

And yet... even blow jobs are highly over-rated when compared to immortality. What most think of as worldly success comes with a long list of expectations and flaming hoops through which one must jump in order to maintain one's imagined success.

When you're on your deathbed, money won't buy you one more breath. You won't be able to fly that private jet to Valhalla, and those squabbling mistresses have squandered all your money so now your 3.5 spoiled nuclear children will have to sell their Ferraris and get a menial job if they want to go to community college. Your wife ran away with your embezzling business partner, and even your dog hasn't noticed you've been gone for the past six weeks while you're lying in the hospital waiting for the brute with the scythe[5] to finish what he started when you committed yourself to what you mistakenly believed would be worldly success.

Did I leave anything out? Ah, yes... if it is your genuine Intent to commit to the path of enlightenment and immortality, the first commitment you have to make is that of 1) recognizing the programming that yanks your puppet strings from dawn till dusk; and 2) learning how to play the game *as if it matters*, Knowing all the while that anything that doesn't advance you toward your Intent is not only meaningless folly, but hatch marks of victory on the bedpost of Death himself. You've been fucked over and left for dead. And such is life in the world of worldly success.

If you really want to get out of life alive, the key is knowing when to hold 'em, knowing when to fold 'em, know when to walk away and when to run... Oh wait... that's Kenny Rogers. But life really *is* a gamble. Learn to play it right.

---

[5] **The brute with the scythe:** Death

The First Fundamental Truth

I find myself being pushed to the edge lately and am keenly seeing some of my character weaknesses and limitations, especially when dealing with other people who may reflect some of these back to me. How does one deal with all this on the path to immortality?

It's important to separate the gnat crap from the pepper. Meaning – are these *really* intrinsic weaknesses or limitations, or are they weaknesses and limitations within the definitions of the program? If someone tells you you're selfish, even if they are right by the definitions of society, is that *really* a weakness or is it a strength in disguise? Refusing to give your energy to the demands of other people might be labeled as 'selfish,' but ultimately it is the ability to say no that gives you back your power.

If you are restricted due to age or illness, is that really a limitation, or is it simply a byproduct of being human which all humans will eventually face if they are fortunate enough to live long enough? Most of the time, the labels others try to pin on you are attempts to manipulate and control you by making you believe you would be a better person if only you would serve *their* needs ahead of your own. Real limitations would consist of conscious choices not to do the work, or to try to convince yourself you are already immortal, such as most religions attempt to do.

You can easily identity limitations by how they manifest. On the Immortal Spirit Forum, we've seen it a few times – would-be seekers who come along believing they have found The Answer, and attempting to shove it up the chute of anyone who is willing to bend over. Those constantly looking for shortcuts or super-powers are confronting two of the greatest obstacles seekers must contend with, because letting go of the delusions one holds about the path is really the first step *on* the path.

We've obviously entertained some genuinely disturbed individuals, and perhaps that isn't surprising. After all, the search for immortality is considered insane by 99.999% of the population, so it stands to reason that those who would be willing to exist in defiance of that "truth" may also be noted to be marching to a different drummer.

The problem is that different drummer is often hammering out a funeral dirge and driving the marcher right off the nearest cliff. Why?

> **The First Fundamental Truth it is simply this: Before you can function and navigate in the immortal realm, you must first be able to function and survive in the mortal realm.**

Those who saunter about with delusions of grandeur or who fall prey to the yammerings of their internal dialog which is telling them they are somehow special and above the law and "we don't need no stinkin' masks" are clearly incapable of playing the game of the dayshine world, which means they would be utterly and fatally lost should they find themselves in the immortal realm.

Am I suggesting that those with serious psychological disorders should abandon the path and get themselves to a nunnery? No. Yes. Maybe. *No.* What I'm saying is that if someone can't play the game convincingly – playing the game *as if* it matters (Self-Stalking 101) – they have failed the first test of a seeker, and until they can overcome whatever disorders might be at work, they will have little success undoing the conditioning that underlies the disorder itself. Yes, some disorders might be classified as organic, but it then becomes a question of which came first – the chicken or the egg, the disorder or the programming that caused it?

And here's the truly ironic part: *If* (and that's a huge word in the sentence I'm about to write)... *If* a seeker's disorder is *strictly* organic, it will tend to disappear *if* that person is somehow – against all odds – successful in attaining the immortal condition. Why? Because once the organic body is eliminated and awareness enters the inorganic state (the Other), all such weaknesses, limitations and disorders of the flesh are no longer present.

But (another tiny word but important here), I have observed that even when a seeker manages to attain the immortal condition under such circumstances, *if* (there it is again) the underlying psychological programming remains, the seeker's trip into the immortal realm will most likely be a short one, because the old programming can't navigate in a milieu where the old rules no longer apply. Another case of the chicken and the egg – no matter *which* came first (the disorder or the underlying cause) – if the programming carries over, the seeker will find themselves adrift and utterly disoriented, usually beyond redemption. Rather like going to sleep in a 21st century bed and waking up in a 25th century world where absolutely nothing is the same, not even the language, the social customs, none of it.

Yes, there might be exceptions, but the problem is that everyone who suffers from such a serious disorder believes *they* are that exception. Chances are... they aren't. Whether the disorder is physical or psychological, it cannot be eliminated by denying its existence – neither in the mortal world or the immortal world.

The Light At the End of the Tunnel
(...is often an oncoming train)

What is enlightenment?

Enlightenment occurs when all the programming, false beliefs and inaccurate conclusions are finally eliminated, leaving a clear beam of awareness stretching from the self into the infinite in all directions and throughout all of "time." This does not imply omniscience, for the enlightened one doesn't suddenly Know everything there is to know. Instead, it indicates the ability to glean what it *needs* to know through that infinite light stretching out to touch and permeate all things.

This is the art of gnosis[6], but again this does not imply the ability to Know the winning lottery numbers or who killed Jimmy Hoffa. It indicates instead a connection to the infinite that is non-local and functions on a synapse of energy that is not located in the brain/mind of the mortal self, but in the inexplicable mystery which is the Other.

An enlightened individual is not necessarily blissful or even particularly serene. The ability to Know comes with equal measures of Dark and Light. And once the Dark is seen and known, it cannot be unseen or unknown. That little-discussed consequence is one primary reason many enlightened individuals swing radically between elation and despair, absolute acceptance and utter outrage.

---

[6] **Silent knowing** (aka gnosis): communication with the higher self and the sentient universe. A state of consciousness accessible through a variety of methods, including Intent, meditation, mind-altering substances such as psilocybin mushrooms, tantric sex, the near-death-experience, sensory deprivation, and many others. Gnosis is the most crucial tool available to the seeker, for the entire knowledge of the entire universe is available. As your abilities and awareness increase, you may begin to have a permanent channel to the voice of gnosis through your connection to the immortal Other.

To be enlightened is to be aware not only of Life, but of its tragically finite nature. Somewhere in that paradoxical elixir is the motivation to live forever, or the decision to welcome mortal death as an alternative to Enlightenment itself.

Proceed at your own risk, for such is the paradox of the mortal realm.

The High Cost of Authenticity
The Path Will Cost You Everything

> *I have only my heart to give.*
> *It is made of starflakes and sea glass.*
> *I pray you break it gently.*

Whenever I have made the statement that this path will cost you everything, it is intended as a dire admonition for anyone who truly believes they are blessed by angels and smiled upon by the gods themselves. What you will discover as you progress in your journey is that another of my statements is equally true: the world really *is* out to get you.

Paranoid? Perhaps. But truth is seldom pretty and perhaps the darkest of the darker teachings is the fact that you stand to lose everything in order to gain one thing.

When I speak of losing everything, it would potentially include not only your material possessions and your loved ones, but whatever it is you hold onto as a comfort zone and functioning belief system. What stands between you and immortality really is everything you think you know, everything and everyone you love, and that includes most of all your own self-imposed matrix – the paradigm that makes you who you are, and at the same time prevents you from ever truly *seeing* who you are. Why? Because the paradigm itself is built upon a false foundation.

If you believe hard work will earn you success, you are probably wrong. If you believe you will attain the immortal condition (or anything else) on the basis of merit, you are definitely wrong. If you believe, 'All things die but it will be different for *me*,' you are as wrong as wrong can be, because the foundational statement itself (all things die) is such that it negates anything that follows in its wake.

So what you really stand to lose is yourself, in the sense that you will no longer be the comfortable companion you've always been to yourself. You will no longer be your own best friend or even your own worst enemy. You will no longer be the class clown who laughs at your bad jokes. You will no longer be the anonymous stranger who gives you a hand job in the shower and promises never to tell.

But for the moment, let's just talk about the world of matter and men.

The first sign of losing everything usually begins with friends and relatives. You've begun to notice that people are really only interested in their own pursuits – which commonly reduces to sex, children, jobs, sex, more sex, and whatever religious dogma they are pretending to uphold despite their debauched lifestyle.

They have no time for your philosophical ponderings about life, death, and the nonexistence of god or any other reasonably compassionate deity. Their talk has turned to diapers and crock pot recipes and the occasional whispers about whoever they are boning that bears no resemblance to their spouse. Your relatives are impatient with you, wondering why you haven't taken that scholarship for a full ride to medical school, never seeming to remember that the mere sight of blood or vomit or poop or needles or a vaginal speculum sends you into a whirlwind of varying exit strategies, for the simple reason that becoming a doctor would first mean agreeing to the first agreement, which states, simply, "All things die."

Humans require agreement and validation, and when you evolve beyond their petty beliefs and even more petty addictions to attention, they come to resent your detachment and the glint of freedom they see in your eyes, and that's when they turn on you, pitchforks and torches at the ready, proclaiming you to be a sinner, a demon, or just a Democrat; and the real reason for all of it is that when one fails to validate *their* consensus, one has become a threat to their fragile status quo.

Your family doesn't know you. Your friends don't have time for you. And gradually you realize that you're spending your Friday nights alone with the cat instead of partying with your mates or even helping your little sister with her algebra homework (not that you understand a single integer of algebra).

Those upon whom you have come to depend for your reference points are no longer at your disposal, and you begin to experience the first major symptom of the path costing you everything.

> **The world begins to blur. It isn't so much that you've lost connection with these phantoms, but you have lost instead your *idea* of yourself in relation to the phantoms and the world they inhabit.**

From there, you usually begin to question why this is a reality and not just one of Mikal's paranoid warnings. "Why *should* the path cost me everything?" you will ask, running down a long list of your achievements and why you are therefore *entitled* to be exempted from the conundrum altogether.

After all, you were winner of the Sixth Grade Spelling Bee, you're a good person, you were chess champion in your freshman year of high school, and you're a good person. You bedded your first virgin at the impressive young age of 14, and did enough weed and

LSD to impress the wandering spirits of Timothy Leary *and* Terence McKenna. In fact, you actually spoke with Mr. Leary in a mushroom-induced vision, and he assured you that you were to be the next guru to the Hollywood stars based on nothing more than your own self-importance. You were destined to become rich, famous, sexually renowned, intellectually idolized, and recipient of a first place trophy presented to you by choirs of angels and endorsed by the Almighty himself. And did you forget to mention that you're a *really* good person?

And yet... here you find yourself in your tiny apartment or your grandmother's basement, depending on the degree of distancing that has occurred thus far, and your justice bone is twitching and in dire need of a splint, because the world at large has abandoned you, without so much as a blind wave from the Queen.

REJECTED

Most seekers quit right about there, not wanting to face the harsh realities now staring them in the face. To go forward means risking even more. How long can you continue to sit in that cubicle all day and listen to Dave one aisle over pontificating on the phone about the health benefits of the Fuck Fat Cellulite Wand, while snickering under his breath at the morons who shell out the money for aforementioned scam device? And don't forget, these are the same imbeciles who then turn up on *your* phone threatening a lawsuit because their

44

thighs are now as big as giant redwoods despite the fact that they've only been eating six cheeseburgers a day instead of the usual ten.

The folly all around you becomes a tangible weight, and though you wonder why the others don't see it, it is painfully clear that they don't, won't, can't, and that is simply *that*. They have not only bought into the bullshit, they are eating it up and pronouncing it sweet! Reviews on Yelp!

The world has lost its veneer of civilization and you *see* right through the illusions, right down into the dirty, vulgar core of it all, and you finally realize that absolutely *nothing* is real and nothing is *un*real and all paths lead nowhere except back to the beginning, and the only winning move is not to play, but you're too far into the game to quit and too awakened to carry on, and it's usually at that point when the world folds in on itself, collapsing like a cheap tent in a storm, and you find yourself utterly and absolutely...

Alone.

Everything you have been taught is a lie. Everything you have believed is a fallacy. The cat still loves you, but you begin to wonder if he's not just jonesing for food rather than genuinely enjoying your company.

What to do?

Nothing to be done.

[[OMG – Mikal did not *just go through that whole ugly diatribe only to conclude with a nihilist statement that it's all just a fart in the wind!]]*

Actually, that is precisely what Mikal did. Because what has to be done is essentially a *not*-doing. The seeker either accepts that the world is folly and her only role is to play the game as if it matters while making every attempt to hold onto the dream of Intent that launched her on the path in the first place; or she folds her wings and drinks the hemlock that will bring her back to the world of matter and men, even if only as a docile zombie looking for some brains.

Those who choose to continue beyond this dark threshold of the abyss do so with the awareness that there are no guarantees one will ever reach the goal Intent has set for them. But one thing is certain: you will *definitely* not reach the goal if you go back to the gaping maw of the matrix and settle into the seductive illusions and delusions of the dayshine continuum.

> **Having lost everything, the seeker comes to *see* that she has lost nothing – because everything was an illusion and a lie to begin with, and one cannot lose what one never really had.**

When the seeker wholly realizes this is when she gains the power and the ability to see the path through, never knowing if she will succeed or fail, but at least knowing she has shed the baggage that would otherwise be the etching on her tombstone.

The path will cost you everything.

If it already has, count yourself among the infinitely blessed.

The Anger Factor

I used to be an easy-going guy but lately it feels like every little thing pisses me off – the anger is out of proportion to the provocation – like I've run out of patience for every ignoranus who ever fell out the back side of a brood mare. No offense to women or fetuses or horses. There has to be something <u>more</u>. (Cue Peggy Lee singing "Is That All There Is?")

This anger syndrome is relatively common among seekers, though I have not observed it to be particularly detrimental unless it becomes an obsessive fixation that might run the risk of obscuring the way. On the other

46

hand, I've worked with apprentices who use their anger as motivation – directing it at the brute with the scythe and projecting themselves as worthy opponents of Death.

As to why the anger begins to manifest in an otherwise "easy-going guy," it is most likely the result of losing the programming that kept you docile and agreeable to things that are hardly agreeable. Once those controlling mechanisms are gone, one of the first indicators can be anger at the fact that you have been lied to and duped since before you were rudely pushed out the back side of that brood mare. The trick, of course, is learning to *direct* the anger rather than allowing it to consume you.

You mentioned *"Is That All There Is?"* Once the blinders fall away, the seeker looks around at the world and realizes there is little if any meaning or purpose to life other than what one brings to it. And bringing meaning and purpose to life itself is rather like taking upon oneself the duties of God without the alien super powers and nifty Batmobile. If that isn't crazy-making, what is?

In one way or another (whether religious programming or social acculturation) you've been subtly conditioned to believe there might be some loving granddad of a deity out there who is going to save you from death, pay your taxes, and bless you with a devoted spouse and 2.5 children you will probably only end up wanting to impale on that white picket fence.

[[OMG – did Mikal just suggest impaling children like Vlad Tepes? What the hell? I don't even <u>have</u> a picket fence!]]

No. Mikal said you would probably *want* to at some point, and if you try to deny that, you are still a prisoner of the delusion that 'happiness' is some inalienable right in a Norman Rockwell painting. But let's stick to the point...

Once you realize with unerring clarity that there is no one to save you or intervene in your piddly mortal affairs (as if God would have nothing better to do than grant wishes all night long like some miscreant genie), it's normal to feel anger, denial, bargaining, depression, and resignation (aka "acceptance.") The five stages of grief kick you in the 'nads and laugh at your pain, often doing a follow-up visit filled with resentment, bitterness and even outright outrage.

For some seekers, the consensual illusions and false beliefs collapse from one moment to the next without any real preparation on your part – and if that has happened, your anger is not only understandable, it is *inevitable*.

> **Seekers who are removing their old foundation *must* replace it with a new one if they are to survive the headlong plunge into the abyss that occurs when Reality and Belief collide like matter and antimatter thrown into a cardboard box together.**

You're angry at the world for *being* the way it *really* is, and you're angry at the deceptions you've been spoon-fed in an attempt to keep you complacent, and you're angry at those who have done the feeding, even if it wasn't conscious or intentional on their part. Well, they *do* know that Santa Claus crap is a lie, and most of them even know their religion is a far worse lie, but the ordinary man who has nowhere to turn for answers tends to fall back on his programming. Easier to go to church every Sunday and hope there is a god, than to summon up his own power of creation and throw off the shackles that bind him to his blindness.

What it really comes down to is that there is no real cure for the anger other than the act of creation itself. Those who sit around feeling sorry for themselves often end up climbing a tall building and taking aim with a high-powered rifle at innocent bystanders in a world without meaning. Those who see that those bystanders aren't at fault are the ones who build towers to heaven – though heaven usually turns out to be what we call Shadowland. The major difference is that Shadowland is an actual energetic structure, a projection of your own creation, whereas heaven is little more than a shared delusion among people who prefer the comfort zone of their pre-existing beliefs to the hard cold push toward immortality.

You've outgrown your cage. Time to throw off the broken bars before they skewer you. Focus the anger into an act of creation. It's often through anger that the Will emerges.

Sex
(..and now that I have your attention)

What about sex? Seems like a lot of mixed messages out there. The Toltecs say sex leaves a hole in the energy body. Some self-proclaimed magi talk about tantric sex being the key that opens the door to the universe. So from an immortal's point of view, where does sex fit into the mix?

For the sake of accuracy, the Toltecs never really said that sex leaves a hole in the energy body, though that could probably be intuited as the end result. The theory is that having children is what creates the hole in the energy body, because the energy required to create life has to come from somewhere, and that somewhere is from the parents themselves. And lest you perpetually horny males think you get a pass on that one because you don't have a womb, think again. The feminine is the fertile ground. The masculine is the seed. Can't have one without the other – at least not quite yet.

I make this distinction because the common concept nowadays is that sex is "just sex." An awkward rubbing together of body parts, often referred to as "bumping uglies," and that's really there all is to it. Your friends have benefits. You rub one out whenever it suits you. You watch so much porn you're keeping the big oil companies in business just to manage the chaffing, and statistically your mind turns toward sex at least a hundred times every day, and that's *if* you believe what I personally think is a conservative estimate.

How does sex fit into a seeker's life? I'm not going to tell you that sex should only be for those who have the good fortune or extreme misfortune to fall in love. And what is love anyway? Some teenagers "fall in love" an average of twice a week, each time believing their pimpled paramour to be the holy soulmate conceived in the embrace of angels and kissed by the lips of God himself.

That's not love. That's sexual obsession at best – perhaps the most powerful force on Earth which guarantees survival of the species by insuring that the brain goes into neutral, the hormones and gonads snap into high gear, and the grunts, groans and wails (largely reflecting disappointment) begin in earnest, and usually last no more than three months until one or both partners are covertly following their genitals in other directions – a direction that inevitably leads to drama, chaos, heartbreak, and a cynicism that shouts, "Love doesn't exist."

[[Wow! Mikal must be one of those celibate assholes! I like sex! Hell, I'd have sex with him just to prove him wrong! Wait – I mean, well, would that make me gay?]]

The thing about sex is that it's a clever trickster who will try to convince you it's the answer to all your prayers. In reality, while sex can benefit a seeker on some levels, it can also become a tremendous albatross *unless* your partner is also a seeker on a parallel path. Hard to find, but not impossible.

50

As for tantric sex, it can have incredible results, propelling mind and energy body into heights of ecstasy and even states of heightened awareness. But here's the thing – most people simply aren't capable of engaging in tantric sex for the same reason they aren't capable of climbing Mt. Everest, or even the stairs leading to their second floor apartment.

Tantric sex, like any other tool, has to be carefully honed and practiced – preferably by yourself until such time as you're not having to holster your gun before you get to the shooting range.

What the serious seeker needs to understand is that sex, like everything else in the mortal realm, requires an expenditure of energy if it's done right. If you want to use sex for magical practices, educate yourself on the practices – then throw all the books out the window and follow your instincts. If your energy and awareness increase, give yourself a pat on the rump and see where it might lead, but don't use it as a substitute for other practices that are equally if not more important.

The real problem many seekers face is learning to separate the act of sex from the state of actual love – for one thing is certain, and that is simply that the two are worlds apart. Sex is a biological function. Love is a universal vibration which connects the seeker to the energetic soul of the infinite. Sometimes the two can coexist in harmony and mutual benefit. Other times sex has been known to single-handedly (left or right hand optional) destroy the seeker when it becomes an all-consuming obsession, as it is actually *designed* to do.

Sex feels good for a reason, though that reason (procreation) has absolutely nothing to do with any potential evolution of mind, body or spirit. In many ways, sex can become the gateway to a lifetime of responsibility and obligation in the form of a house in the suburbs teeming with rugrats, curtain climbers, and a spouse who comes home later and later every night, and eventually doesn't come home at all. That syndrome starts somewhere, and all too often that's in the back seat of a Camaro (not particularly comfortable, I can tell you).

So think carefully and choose wisely. *If* you want a life that consists of the white picket fence and a golden lab in the yard and a cat or two in the bay window, chances are you can have it in some manner of speaking; but if you *do* choose that route, chances are very high that you won't be able to maintain the commitment to your journey because even though energy itself is limitless, *time* is not. At least not while you are still mortal.

It's right about here that I'm expected to say something uplifting and rose-colored about sex. And I could. Sex can be a life-altering experience – but the question becomes whether that alteration will be beneficial or detrimental to the goals of your long-term Intent. I'm far from any Puritanical evangelist urging celibacy. On the other hand, I've seen too many seekers derailed by what amounts to a one-night-stand that turns into a soul-cage from which there is very little possibility of escape.

If you are one of those rare individuals who can engage in sexual encounters without forming deep-rooted emotional attachments, then bone away and be sure to carry a good supply of condoms. But the nature of sex is that it is genetically *designed* since the dawn of time to engender feelings of affection and commitment – aka "falling in love."

Now don't give me that look. You're not immune, nor should you be. Falling in love for the right reasons is the most wondrous and mystical experience you will ever know. Love really *is* the reason for all things. Just don't mistake the hormonal rush that comes from sex as any indicator of true love. See it for what it is rather than for what you've been conditioned to believe, for clarity is really your only ally in the fight against sexual obsession or sexual addiction.

Am I exaggerating? Depends on what you want out of life that will determine how you approach the subject of sex, both as a physical activity and a philosophical conundrum.

The Universal Conundrum
Primal forces in direct opposition

When a seeker becomes over-confident it has been observed that obstacles can begin to appear in that seeker's path – anything from minor inconveniences to catastrophic illness or worse. This is an interesting phenomenon, since the universe is sentient but not concerned with the machinations of individuals. It doesn't act as a purveyor of punishment or reward; it isn't god; it cares not one wit what you do or don't do.

However, it also appears there is a naturally-occurring phenomenon which amounts to the simultaneous promotion-of and hindrance-to evolution. Meaning: the universe is designed to provide every seeker with every possible opportunity to evolve, but at the same time it will seemingly block or thwart that same evolution as if to force the individual to overcome almost insurmountable odds.

To illustrate, it looks something like this:

You're skipping down the road with a happy-hippie grin on your face, 5 grams of psilocybe cubensis mushrooms in your pocket for the oncoming night's shamanic journey intended to propel you into your instantaneous transmogrification[7]; and your Other is whispering naughty suggestions of eternity in your ear.

---

[7] **Transmogrification**: a transference of all life energy (consciousness, awareness, individuated memory) from its mortal human coil into its immortal energy body (aka "The Other"). Because the Other is a quantum state, it may take any form, and may change form at will. Transmogrification is the process through which the mortal seeker attains the immortal condition. It is considered the highest form of transformation, since it is directed and willed by the seeker *prior* to physical death.

All is right with all the worlds. And yet, you abruptly trip over an unseen obstacle in the road and fall face first into the path of an oncoming Toyota, breaking several bones and damaging multiple internal organs in the process. While searching for your ID, the cop who comes to your aid finds your mushrooms and places you under pending arrest, assuming you survive the six surgeries necessary to save your now-miserable life.

Your Other can only look on from the sidelines, because ultimately the mortal's fate is in the mortal's hands, and as you lie there in the ambulance listening to the warbling siren that sounds all too much like a dragon's death wail, you realize that every step you have ever taken, every thought you've ever entertained, literally *everything* you've ever done has led you to *this* moment.

It's not your fault, you tell yourself.

And that's where the universal conundrum kicks in. It is often the seekers who have been the most diligent, the most focused, the most determined, who are the very ones to find themselves swatted down by the fickle hand of Fate, knowing all the while that there's really no such thing as Fate; and so the irony is even more ironic and difficult to digest while some 220 pound hominid is pounding on your chest and forcing air into your lungs with something that looks like a deformed blue football and smells like a diseased crotch.

You've made your bed and now you must lie in it. Your friends (assuming you still have any friends) can only hope that bed isn't a coffin, because they really have better things to do next week than attend your funeral and draw straws to determine which of the unlucky bastards has to take guardianship of your yappy little dog, (appropriately named Toto), as outlined in the friendship clause in your will.

Some speculate that this phenomenon occurs because the universe functions under the metaphysical law which, loosely defined, says that if self-willed

54

evolution were easy or practical, it would not really be a forward-mutation of the self, but simply a natural progression from one phase into the next. While it isn't possible to fully comprehend the possible logic of this see-saw syndrome, it is virtually impossible not to observe it in action.

The other interesting aspect of this is that when a seeker denounces the path and returns to the comfort zone of the program, the obstacles generally diminish or vanish altogether. And so it comes as no surprise that many seekers who find themselves treading freezing waters in the abyss might indeed accept the life-vest thrown down by the phantoms on the road to Ixtlan[8].

Does this happen to every seeker? Some say yes, others disagree. From my own observations over a long period of time, I have seen that it is most likely to affect those who are closing in on transmogrification, for one thing is certainly certain: once a seeker achieves the immortal condition, the phantoms have lost the battle, the powers that be are rendered powerless, and the seeker has moved beyond the ability of death to undo.

This is a complex and, in many ways, indecipherable conundrum. When seekers attempt to put human understanding onto a universal quandary, the end result is generally one of confusion, frustration and even anger.

The best approach is to observe and learn through experience rather than trying to second-guess the universe. It could even be said that the only way to muddle through the conundrum is to use *the force* – which not only exists, but is the seeker's ally in

---

[8] **Phantoms on the road to Ixtlan:** a reference to the works of Carlos Castaneda, wherein it is observed that seekers (warriors) are often seduced by well-meaning phantoms (friends, family members, kindly strangers) whose agenda is to "help" the seeker come back to the real world. "Come with us," they say. "We have food, shelter, and a big flat-screen tv." Without doubt, any seeker who has been on the path for more than a day has met a few of these brain-eating zombies.

navigating the predatory universe. That "force" is the power of silent knowing, the voice of gnosis.

Abandon Hope
(It's your only hope!)

You talk a lot about unconditional love, intent and will being powerful tools in a seeker's bag of tricks, but I'm wondering how you would classify the things that might be a seeker's undoing. I keep banging my head against a wall of uncertainty, thinking that the <u>next</u> time I turn the corner my twin will be standing there. I don't necessarily mean literally but like I'm going to cross the crossroads and something is going to change other than my underwear changing from day to day. But then I look around and realize I'm running in place, chasing after a pretty light that's just a symptom of a brain aneurism.

So what do you think about the things that plug us up and give seekers mental and spiritual constipation?

At the very least, I can say you have a dark but altogether necessary sense of humor.

This conundrum you speak of answers to the name of hope, and though most new age gurus try to sell it in the form of good vibrations, positive thinking, and expensive retreats to exotic locations, hope is one of the single most destructive "emotions" in the range of human experience. I'm not entirely convinced hope is an emotion as much as it is a default mechanism humans have to keep them from hurling themselves into the snapping jaws of the abyss.

And yet, it has been observed that only when a seeker loses all hope do they have any real possibility of embracing a solution that has nothing to do with some airy-fairy placebo being shoved up their chute by the purveyors of platitudes swiped from the pages of *The Secret* or other texts promising success, happiness and true love in exchange for nothing more than hope in the heart and – more realistically – air between the ears.

Am I saying it's wrong to hope things will get better? Not necessarily, but hope is one of those things that only tends to manifest when action is taken to bring about the desired results. Hoping for things to get better won't do much good to the jobless couch potato who spends his day watching reruns of *I Love Lucy* in his grandma's basement while lamenting the fact that he's still a virgin at the age of 47. Much as no one really wants to believe it, hope is the thought from which action must be taken – but without the action, hope is nothing more than a dark and dangerous predator, sucking away at one's lifeforce.

Many people have told me, "I'm living on hope." If that's the case, they aren't really living. They are only waiting for some idea (probably not even clearly formed) to spring into being because it is wished-for. They are waiting for a miracle, and though miracles do happen, they are rare and unpredictable at best.

The only real cure for what you are experiencing is forward motion. Even if you don't know where you're going, take the next step in the direction of your dreams. If you feel you are stuck at a crossroads, choose a direction and see where it leads. Occasionally, hope can transform into Intent, which often occurs when all hope is actually abandoned altogether.

If you genuinely feel held in stasis, it might not matter *what* direction you choose. The important thing is to know that while you're going nowhere, the clock is ticking and hope might be the glue keeping your feet from moving.

If you feel spiritually constipated, relentless Intent is the only laxative.

Hope is a cruel bitch wearing a pretty dress. This isn't really a serious question but why do we have hope when it seems like pretty much everything is hopeless?

The question might not be intended seriously, but it is nonetheless worthy of exploration. The universe is a master of opposites and paradoxes. I have always been a fan of the story of the fox and the grapes. It certainly seems that many things exist which are placed just out of reach – whether to serve as motivation, inspiration or desperation, who's to say?

I have wondered over the centuries if hope is the Mother of Intent – and while that is perhaps a more optimistic view than many would expect from this wily old wizard, it is the only semi-rational explanation I have formulated. If we hope to fly, we must either grow wings or build them out of metal and jet fuel. If we hope to go the stars, we must either construct a starship or figure out a way to get abducted by aliens. If we hope for immortality, we must push the boundaries of what is believed to be possible into the realm of what is most often perceived to be *im*possible.

Otherwise, if hope is *not* the Mother of Intent, it is the Father of Lies – promising the stars but delivering only grave dust. In earlier times, many prophets were executed lest they sing their prophecies into being; and though that may seem a drastic and cruel solution, it did have a certain poetic justice in spite of itself.

What to do about hope? Hope it isn't another manifestation of Agent Smith. It may well be. It may well not be.

I hope for the best.

What is the Ultimate Key to Know Oneself?

Before you can know who you *are*, you must first learn to *see* who you are *not*. This is where the practice of stripping away the false beliefs and deeply imbedded programming begins – questioning not just *what* you believe but *why* you believe it. Though this is something I have said countless times, it will always bear repeating because the real issue faced by most humans – even most seekers – is that they believe they are the end product of their beliefs, when in reality it is those beliefs that prevent them from knowing the true identity of the face that hides behind the mask in the mirror.

So the next inevitable question becomes one of *how* does the diligent seeker know what's *real* and what is only a false conviction masquerading as truth?

There are some exercises (*don't everyone run away at once – no treadmill or Atlas machine required*) that can help determine the difference between what you believe and what simply *is*. And though I have previously had an agreement with myself not to offer blanket exercises to those who might not be ready for the outcome, I will now exercise my right to be fickle, change my mind, and do it anyway, because if someone *really* isn't ready to come face to face with their authenticity, they will throw the book over their shoulder, decide firmly that Mikal is a soothsayer and not a truthsayer, and that will simply be that.

The agenda here is to initiate a conversation with your authentic self – which is a lot harder than you might think.

Sit or stand in front of a mirror and voice out loud the question, "What is my most deeply-held belief?"

Not surprisingly, you will get the auto-fill responses first, but if you are properly dogged in your practices, they will eventually give up when rejected a sufficient number of times, not unlike a fickle teenage suitor.

When you feel you can be honest with yourself (also harder than you can imagine) begin to examine the things you hold most dear. Is it a belief in God? A trust in the government (not likely if your IQ is above room temperature)? Do you believe you were Marie Antoinette in a past life (and therefore you believe in reincarnation, which ultimately means you believe you will have "another chance" if you fail in your bid for immortality)?

Whatever you discover to be your most deeply-held belief, now ask yourself, *Where did this belief originate?* Almost always you'll recall that somewhere along the way, someone outright told you what you should believe about ___ (fill in the blank).

You might even hear that moment captured in memory in that person's voice, at which point you might want to ask the pesky aural apparition where *they* came to believe whatever it is they're peddling; and again it will be an echo from someone *they* knew and probably trusted, though seldom if ever do *any* of these sources have any ability to provide evidence to substantiate their beliefs.

They just... *believe.* The Sunday School teacher told them God is watching over them. So they believe it. The doctor told them they have the genetic markers for cancer. And so they believe it regardless of the conflicting belief that God is watching over them. The dude in that martial arts movie said he was Buddha's handmaiden in a previous incarnation. And so *you* believe it, which comes with a whole cartload of manure that will eventually spill over and bury you in the avalanche. Namely – by inadvertently admitting to yourself that you believe in reincarnation, you also accept the accompanying addendum which is often sung in the voice of some annoying ginger kid yowling off-key, "Tomorrow, tomorrow, there's always tomorrow!"

And you believe it, even if you don't believe you believe it.

And yet...

60

At some point in your early life, didn't your mother ask you that all-important question that comes pre-loaded with all mothers everywhere? *If everyone else jumped off a skyscraper, would you do it, too?*

Maybe you would. But guess what? You don't *really* have super powers. You aren't the reincarnation of Bruce Lee or Bruce the shark, and maybe you will finally start to *see* that when you get serious enough with your practices to question all those things you never dared to question before.

And only then will you begin to see *why* you've never questioned your sacrosanct beliefs previously. When they fall, they take whole worlds with them – worlds you have built in your mind and, yes, in your now-broken heart.

Here the third eye begins to open, though you will probably need some Visine and an aspirin or two before you're ready for the next step, because what you *now* have to consider are the really hard questions that are sure to yank the rug out from under you and sizzle the foundation you've been standing on all your life.

How do these beliefs safeguard the status quo of the consensual reality?

Ah, and it's right about here that you start to *see* just how steadfastly you yourself have upheld and substantiated the consensual agreement of the dayshine world as much as any corporate executive with his 3-piece suit and leather briefcase.

But I'll stop here and let you have that head-on collision with reality for yourself – and don't doubt for a moment that this is one of the deepest channels of the rabbit hole, the one that has sucked you in and is loathe to let you go.

And finally...

How do your most sacred beliefs protect your own comfort zones?

The answers might well be more frightening than Voldemort's wand, but it's important you look them squarely in the face and *see* them for what they truly are.

> **Beliefs are the bedrock of the consensual world, deeply embedded into the brick, stone, and mortar that hold reality together. For as long as your beliefs are intrinsic to that mix, _you_ are the glue holding the devil's horns in place and providing the brute with the scythe job security for the duration of time itself.**

It's all about you.

Or, more accurately, it's about the masked man in the mirror who's been obscuring you from yourself until this moment.

If you are truthful with yourself, these simple exercises are the C-4 that will end the world as you've known it. But again, to be accurate, it will only end the world as you *believe* you've known it.

From the ruins of that devastation, you are presented with the seeker's ultimate choice: rise up from the ashes with eyes wide open, or pull the covers over your head and try to tie the mask back in place.

It's up to you. It always has been.

Collapse of Civilization?
...or escape from the matrix?

To what extent do you think civilization as we know it is on the brink of collapse? And what would that mean to any seekers who might be among the survivors – or would there even be any survivors?

From my observations, civilization has been on the brink of collapse since the first two cavemen decided to play cards on Friday nights and began inviting others of their individual covens to join in. Perhaps this went well

62

for a time, allowing the lovely cave people to form alliances and work together toward common goals. Building saddles for all those dinosaurs obviously required group effort, and then riding those dinosaurs into battle against neighboring tribes of rivals to secure exclusive rights to the watering hole also required joint effort, and so civilization sprang into being right along with wars and fears and suspicions and hatred and bigotry, even though the watering hole was sufficiently large enough to accommodate all the cave people *and* their thirsty dinosaurs.

It was an agreement – like all civilizations ultimately are – but agreements are fragile and based on a trust that is difficult if not impossible to maintain. Eventually somebody cheats at cards or does the zugg-buggering mating dance with somebody else's wife or husband or dinosaur, and the allies of today become the enemies of tomorrow, and friends become rivals, and lovers betray lovers until eventually the whole agreement falls apart and both sides start secretly pissing in the watering hole until it becomes contaminated beyond any possibility of recovery.

The cave people and all the animals become sick, and many die of some "invisible disease," never realizing even for a moment that it was their own actions that created the disease that finally kills the majority of them.

But just in case the disease missed some, along comes the comet to rid the planet of those pesky dinosaurs who have now begun eating the sickly cave people, because all of their natural prey *also* became sick from the polluted water and died, so Zugg and Ling-Lang might be crunchy and not have a lot of meat on their bones, but to a hungry T-rex that hardly seems much of an inconvenience.

So while all the dinosaurs are standing in the rain, stomping in the mud to create a *new* watering hole, they are wiped out in an instant by the comet because God needed that piece of real estate to set up landscaping for the savage Garden of Eden, and the rest is history (even if slightly revised now and then to suit the historians and the politicians and the popes and princes and all the king's men who still insist on believing cavemen rode dinosaurs).

Skip forward about 5,000 or 5 billion years (depending on which mythical His-story you choose to believe) and here we are on the brink of yet another collapse of the agreement. It has obviously collapsed more than a few times along the way. Atlantis. Lemuria. Ancient Greece. The Roman Empire. The library at Alexandria. The Jedi. Hogwarts.

And in each of those instances, the remaining survivors rebuilt the agreement, perhaps basing it on different rules or ideals, but nonetheless civilization as it has always been is little but a consensus – the truths and lies to which humans agree to agree. Break the rules and risk the wrath of the Sith or the madness of some lunatic in the White House with his stubby finger on the nuclear trigger. Sleep with someone else's sheep and risk strawberry rotfoot, except it might not be your foot that is rotting off. The dark possibilities are endless.

The agreement is extremely fragile, as you already know if you've been paying attention for the short span of time you've been riding the third rock from the sun.

Using the 2020 Covid-19 fiasco as an example, perhaps the biggest agreement of all is to pretend there is sufficient tangible collateral backing up all that money people are worried about while their businesses are shut down and their children are sick and their sheep hasn't come home in a fortnight. But instead of tending the garden to create a remedy for the kids, or combing the brothels looking for that whoring sheep, the humans scamper about clutching their hands to their heads, squawking about the economy or the suppression of their freedom, but secretly *far* more concerned about the fact that they are being prevented by circumstances from banging their mistress or the cabana boy than they are about any actual and factual concern.

The agreement isn't real.

The agreement *can't* be real because it is based on mutual distrust and the inherent human proclivity to self-interest. Many fine-sounding words may be spoken by all the posers and pretenders, but at the end of the day, nobody is going to give you their last roll of toilet paper. Or even if they do (ain't gonna happen, but let's speculate), even if they *do*... they are going to want something in return that you probably can't give or *won't* give, and so the friendly Friday night card game turns into a skirmish that quickly escalates into a war as each side calls forth their bannermen and the waving of flags and the game of thrones begins in earnest, just one more pandemic of hate and fear and distrust brought on by some twatwaffle who thought the ace up his sleeve would protect him from the comet.

Will there be any survivors? Of course. There always are – but whether that's a good thing remains to be seen, and so far it's not looking promising. Will seekers be among the survivors? Of course. They always are. Will they rise up to build a new and better agreement with a new and better civilization? Let's hope not, because seekers more than anyone else should realize that the agreement is not sustainable and therefore a new paradigm will have to emerge if there is *ever* to be any manner of utopian society on this planet or any other.

But there's a catch-22 that should be obvious.

> **True seekers recognize that you can't save the world, you can only save yourself. And saving yourself doesn't include trying to set up any utopian societies or guiding the sheeple to the night light.**

At best, it involves practicing what the Toltecs referred to as "the right way to live[9]." And if you don't know what that means by now, I'd wager you are probably not a true seeker. That doesn't mean you can't be. It only means you need to figure it out before your ego eats a hole in your reason and convinces you you're the next messiah.

The real trick to survival is *seeing* civilization for what it is and what it isn't. To the human perspective, it is a broad agreement, characterized by the 10 commandments just as an example of what you're agreeing to. Don't kill. Don't fuck your neighbor's dog. Don't steal milk from the baby or the cat. The usual rules and regs.

From an immortal perspective, civilization is little more than a fragile and temporary game wherein the humans set forth a lot of lofty ideals (The Constitution of the United States, the Magna Carta, the Rules of Hoyle, and so on) and actually believe they are going to live according to them. Inevitably they fail – not because their intentions aren't good, but because there will always be rule breakers and sheep-fuckers and those who cheat at cards.

---

[9] **The right way to live:** A concept put forth by don Juan in the writings of Carlos Castaneda. The right way to live is a code of ethics embedded in the heart and soul of all living things. It has nothing to do with morality or religion or beliefs. It is the simple awareness that killing the pregnant buffalo diminishes the herd and threatens the future for one's own tribe, for example.

The Meaning of Life, the Price of Death

Does life have any meaning or purpose? We've heard all the nice pat phrases, like God answers all our prayers, never abandons us, never gives us problems we cannot solve, and so on. Then you encounter the concentration/death camps – Treblinka and Auschwitz, for example What then? Explain that!

I cannot tell you there is any definitive *meaning* of life. If there is, it is entirely personal to each individual. Some might say life's meaning is family. Others find meaning in various causes – environmental, political, religious. But again, all of those things are purely subjective rather than universal, and perhaps that's as it should be, since a diverse experience of life opens the door to infinite possibilities rather than providing standardized answers for the masses, which would only encourage stagnation.

As for meaning? None of it means *anything* in the grand scheme of the Everything. On the other hand, it means everything to the stray kitten you pluck from the gutter and give a forever home. It means everything to the stranger whom you just casually reach out to prevent from stepping in front of a bus. It means everything to the spider you catch on your computer monitor and relocate on a bush outdoors instead of squashing her flat.

Meaning isn't found just by virtue of being alive. It is found – or, more accurately, it is *created* – through your actions. But with that said, none of those actions – no matter how selfless or profoundly good – are going to save the world or even be remembered.

Therefore, any meaning that may exist is within yourself. If you do good deeds because you think you should, you are probably wasting your time and, worse, your energy. If you are doing good deeds thinking they will earn you brownie points with God, you are *definitely* wasting your time and energy. The actions you take have to be taken with the awareness that they are for *you.*

Regarding the topic of purpose, what I have observed is that the purpose of life is evolution itself. Not just on a grand scale, but particularly as it applies to individuals struggling to rise above the programming in order to embrace a more enlightened perspective of life, death, and everything in between.

With regard to Treblinka and Auschwitz, clearly these were the designs of human madmen, and not part of any divine plan. If you look back through all of history, or if you happen to have the advantage of having witnessed some of it personally, what you will quickly *see* is that humans are absolute masters of mayhem, and for absolutely *no* reason other than inherent sadism and personal prejudices of one sort or another.

Certainly there was nothing logical or rational about the crimes of the Holocaust. There was no meaning and no purpose whatsoever – just human nature living down to its lowest common denominator, using the tools of fear and emotional manipulation to control the masses. And yet... control them for *what?* Obviously even that explanation doesn't entirely hold water, so we have to look at the unthinkable – the only purpose was to exterminate one group of people in order to satisfy the certifiably insane desires of a single individual.

From a strictly spiritual perspective, things of this nature are as far removed from Spirit as it is possible to be. Those who enact such crimes upon others are always power-hungry lunatics who seek to be remembered, even if for all the wrong things. It is the only form of "immortality" they will ever know.

> **A man who has no soul cannot see any value in the souls of others, and in fact resents and despises what others have that he lacks within himself.**

The Holocaust and other similar events throughout history are the desperate acts of desperate men and women. Death camps are clearly manifestations of the very worst thing of which humans are capable – for anything that robs another of their life is not only heinous beyond all comprehension, it is also energetically sufficient to rob those who do it of any possibility of evolution – not because any god or deity is keeping score, but because moving in contradiction to the universe itself tends not to end well for those who choose that path. Their component atoms will be redistributed to become obsolete auto parts and meaningless graffiti on the walls of whatever Hell might exist, even if it is only right here on Earth.

And for the sake of completeness and absolute clarity, the same fate awaits anyone who willfully abuses animals, children, or any other living thing. Your free will ends where someone else's right to life begins. Doubt it at your own peril.

Depression: The Bastard Offspring

Seems like everyone I meet is fighting depression. You've been on the planet longer than most, so what I want to know is whether depression has always been here and people just didn't talk about it until Facebook became the world's diary.

And not just what is depression, but why is it such an epidemic? Do immortals endure depression or is it strictly a human disorder?

It is true I come from what has been called a simpler time. And while the complexities of mortal life might have been fewer, the level of difficulty was the same, and as a result the efforts required for survival were such that one was exhausted by the end of a day of farming or hunting/gathering, and had very little time or energy left over to lie awake in bed pondering the unjust nature of the universe.

What I observed in those simpler times was that as a person aged and less was demanded of him physically (younger family members took over the tasks of hunting/gathering and so forth), the man might then lean toward depression or even despair as he confronted the realization that he was no longer useful to the family, the community, or even to himself – all of which might be erroneous conclusions, but nonetheless weighed heavily on his mind due to the underlying programming which taught that a man *must* be productive.

As a result of such thoughts, the man would begin to withdraw from loved ones – who were too busy working the fields to pay him much attention anyway – and by the time he had been retired for no more than a year, he had slipped into what is now commonly called depression.

Whenever I asked individuals in this situation about their melancholy, the most common response – when they were honest – pointed at the fact that the man had worked all his life; raised his children, who were now tasked with the burden of caring for him; believed (albeit reluctantly at times) in a benevolent creator-god; and yet despite all his kind deeds and selfless work, his life was behind him and short of Elijah's reprieve in the form of a fiery chariot coming down from heaven, he would soon take his final breath and lie forever beneath the very soil he had tilled. Life would go on without him.

Even though instructed by well-meaning preachers that he should find great comfort and joy in being taken by God to sit at his feet, the man found no such relief, for by this time he had recognized the lies for what they were, and his greatest regret was that he hadn't seen it sooner so that he might have had at least some minor possibility of finding some other way out of a maze which now appeared to have only one fatal exit.

Mortality.

Nothing has really changed since those simpler times, and mortality is at the root of most cases of depression, even if the one suffering it doesn't recognize that fact. *Tick tock, tick tock.* "Shorter of breath, and one day closer to death[10]."

Obviously there are many forms of depression. Some are situational and therefore transient – such as what occurs with the loss of a loved one. Other forms are more obscure, seeming to have no immediately obvious reason, but which usually track in one way or another to the victim's awareness of their own finite nature.

Some say depression is death's premature calling card – a reminder that the brute is coming for you eventually, and to live life now and to the fullest *because* it is finite. Others say depression is merely the inevitable acceptance that occurs when one realizes (or comes to believe) there is no way out except through the cemetery gates.

---

[10] "Time" by Pink Floyd

Depression is the
bastard offspring of a finite life.

In response to your second question – immortals may or may not harbor depression, and for the same reasons. Not that they themselves are battling mortality, but quite often someone they care about remains stubbornly human and so the immortal knows the grief to come as well as the darkness that accompanies going on without someone you love. Not with any expectations of "We will meet again." But quite literally with the knowledge that the day of "till death do us part" has arrived.

Yes, immortals can experience depression, though it is more along the lines of a somber melancholy as opposed to the traditional definition of environmental depression.

―――

We make our home
where goblins dare not travel,
somewhere near the banks of Styx,
suckling the breast of immortal grief
while the ferryman counts his coins.

Drama

The brute with the scythe is the greatest Drama teacher ever to exist.

As long as you are taking instruction from him, you can learn nothing from me...

...or anyone else.

Your statement here is short, bittersweet, and to the point. But what does it really mean?

Drama is the great destroyer of seekers because it is addictive. It will always be easier to dig a grave than build a stairway to heaven. It will always be more entertaining to dwell on negative pleasantries than to practice impeccability.

Drama comes in all shapes and sizes and in all walks of life and death. Most are deeply rooted in what I have referred to as negative pleasantries – the state that exists when someone secretly thrives on certain types of conflict and might be responsible for perpetrating or at least exacerbating conflict and drama as a means to avoid doing the real work of the path.

Examples? Too many to list, but a few common ones might include:

1. Frequent or ongoing conflict with a coworker or family member – knowing what buttons to push and leaning on them to create a drama for whatever reasons one might care to create a drama. Common lines of dialog among the actors might be, "She started it!" "He called me a twat!" "She seduced my goat!"

Petty bullshit, in other words. And always – most important to note – *always* served on a golden platter of self-righteousness. *Righteous.* The need to be right even when you are clearly wrong. Conflict and drama for no reason other than the care and feeding of your sad little ego.

2. The "yebbut" syndrome. If you ask someone for advice and then argue with the words "Yes, but..." that's creating drama. Thank them for their input and walk away with your righteousness clutched in your right hand, stroking as you go.

Generating conflict through passive-aggressive arguments is a prime example of unnecessary drama. This is especially true when you know the advice you received is correct, but you don't want to take it because it would be inconvenient and interfere with your goal to watch every single video on Pornhub.

News flash: *no one cares what you do or don't do.* If you ask for advice and don't take it, it's your walk to walk. Maybe you're right. Maybe you're wrong. The First Fundamental Lie[11] is keeping score and as the old story goes, "Time will tell."

3. "My dog died." I once asked an apprentice to write a short essay on the subject of immortality, why it appealed to her, and what programs and belief systems she thought she might have to overcome. I had given no specific deadline, other than "next time we connect," which was usually about once a month. A month went by... nada. Two months. Nothing. Three months. I asked if she had thought about it, at which point she became extremely defensive, hands on hips, confrontational pose, and led with the words, "My dog died! Not that you asked!"

Interesting approach, no? How was I to know her dog died? I didn't know she even *had* a dog. Her

---

[11] **The First Fundamental Lie**: The human paradigm is built on the false notion of Time, and so it could be observed by one outside of the matrix that the entire paradigm itself is erroneous because it has created within its subjects a viewpoint that is based on what immortals call The First Fundamental Lie. You are made of the pixels and photons of limitlessness and timelessness, yet unable to access that nature because the agenda of any consensus is to create parameters which can only limit the power and understanding of the thing itself.

response was an intentional attempt to create drama and conflict, while simultaneously attempting to evade a simple task I had given her – not for *my* benefit, but for her own assimilation.

Obviously if she could create a conflict with me wherein she believed she had the upper hand (her dog died, after all), then anything I might say would be deemed irrelevant in comparison to her pain and suffering. Maybe some truth to that... *if* she even had a dog. I later found out it was her neighbor's dog who died and so she had become a liar as well as a drama queen. She was no longer an apprentice after that.

Drama is what one does to avoid doing everything else. These are just random examples. Look around. You'll see plenty more every day. If you play into the fight, you've already lost the war.

I'm experiencing a lot of drama lately in my own life but it's 90% my fault.

If that's a true statement – that it's 90% your fault – then it's 100% your *responsibility* to take charge of whatever situation exists and make it work to your advantage rather than letting it derail you while simultaneously eating you alive.

There are times when it is better to humble oneself on the stage of the play, rather than have the play become real to the extent that it becomes all-consuming. I've known men who offended a king and refused out of misguided pride to apologize or offer recompense. Their tombstones often read, "He stood his ground." Admirable. ...right up until the guillotine took his head.

I get your point, but it's hard to know what to do. Does a seeker get involved in worldly causes or not?

Depends on what you want on your tombstone.

Resurrecting the Self

Is there anything we can do to breathe life back into the world? Just seems that wherever I look, everything is going to Hell in a handbasket, to use an old cliché.

The world at large has lost its soul. When that occurs, the collapse of social order isn't far behind. It doesn't mean the end of the world or the destruction of humanity; it only means a decadent and cruel environment where there is no regard for the individual and no appreciation for the artists, visionaries, and truthsayers.

Interests have shifted from personal or spiritual to technological and self-indulgent. Most humans today do not believe in any sort of spirit. If asked, many will tell you, "We live and we die. That's all there is." And for them, that has become the reality. When the soul dies, the *search* for the soul ceases and reality is created according to the lowest common denominator beliefs.

People began living solely in a plasticized world comprised of the pixels of reason sometime during the late 20th Century. All sense of wonder and awe and even love were traded in for the latest iPhone or the most expensive gaming computer. The animals wept. The stars closed their eyes. The rivers ceased to inspire poets. And the world slowly died.

You ask what you can do to breathe life back into it? The only way I know is the salvation and resurrection of your Self – the part of you that is real and whole and eternal beyond this fragile transient manifestation. That is the road to your individuated immortality – the choice that leads to being more than the sum of your organic, mortal components.

Life as you presently know it can end – either on a personal level known as death, or on a global level which has already been set in motion. And yet, *you* are the catalyst and the cocoon from which Love and Life will always return.

Technology is a tremendous distraction, but it is really only the underlying program that encourages the distraction. It's certainly possible to live without so much technology, but in the society that currently exists, it is not convenient, so the trick is learning to turn the cell phone off, limit gaming to no more than an hour a day (I hear the banging of pitchforks and the scent of lit torches moving in my direction), walk away from Facebook, Tweeter, and all other social media when it has become nothing more than an indulgence, and *take responsibility* for your relationship with technology. Most simply can't – or won't.

A recent article I read compared the addiction to social media as being equal to that of heroin or heavy smoking. It was described as a habit that triggers the addiction areas of the brain and lures its victims into complacency just as mythical sirens once lured sailors to their deaths on the rocks. According to myth, the wise sailors learned to use earplugs. The rest perished.

Many seekers have said they feel they were born into the wrong era. And yet, is there any *right* era? The past has a certain nostalgic allure to it, but you would not enjoy the black plague or the Nazi regime or the harsh rule of petulant boy kings. You are exactly where you need to be. Or even if not, you are where you have landed and there are no return flights.

The hardest part of the journey is realizing it *is* solitary. But it doesn't have to be without love. In that regard, the trick is finding someone who loves the silence and the solitude and the pain as much as you do – not someone who will become dependent on you, or be so needy you will want to strangle them, but someone who stands by your side with the same passion you possess, even if it is of a dark and painful nature at times.

The Chaos and the Clutter

In re-reading <u>Teachings of the Immortals</u>, *I came across this passage that continues to haunt me. I'm wondering if my reasons for pursuing this path are strong enough to be sustainable, or if I'm only grasping at it like a lifeboat for fear nothing else is out there. I've had more than one obsession over the years, but none of them have really lasted.*

> "It is as simple as this: you either want to live forever or die at the end of this short mortal season, and either reality is determined entirely by the manner in which you live. You can have other pleasures but not other obsessions, for the truth is that if you're devoting more thought and energy to the things of dust, you are choosing to assemble your own death, and it should come as no surprise that the brute with the scythe makes the taste of such things powdered-sugar pleasing."
>
> – *Teachings of the Immortals*

While this concept is vitally important to all seekers, it was written to someone who wanted to be an apprentice of mine, yet someone who had cluttered her life with all manner of noise and chaos, to such an extent that she was one of the most fragmented individuals I had ever encountered. In the beginning, perhaps her desire to engage the path was genuine, but it was clear to see that before she could do so in any sort of productive fashion, she would have to let go of some of that clutter.

I will state emphatically that this path is not easy or straightforward under the best of circumstances. It is not for everyone. In fact, it is not for most, even those who originally believe they might want to choose it. It's as I've said before – *the path chooses you, not the other way around.*

I encourage all seekers to pursue their creativity, whether in the form of music or writing or art or whatever it might turn out to be. It is through creativity that one connects with the Other, for it is often the wild, zinging spark of elation that comes with creativity that awakens and strengthens the connection between the self and the Other. Even most immortals continue to create on some level, for it is the act of bringing something into being that did not exist before that is the energetic underpinnings of manifestation.

I peck holes in the shiny black egg
hoping for a glimpse of Something More,
knowing all along
the stars are only porch lights
on the gates of Hell,
designed to attract
distracted moths.

The problems arise when one becomes addicted to the creative process to such an extent that it can become an obsession that really doesn't enhance the living of life, but can begin to consume and subsume it. This was the issue with my wannabe apprentice.

She was addicted to the "high" of whatever she was doing, and to such an extent that the *pursuit* of the high became the focus of her existence rather than the pursuit of her own growth and evolution. Whenever she would hit even a minor snag in the path, she would throw her hands in the air and proclaim she didn't understand, or declare herself as remedial, and it was ultimately this self-degradation that ate a hole in her heart and caused her to run-not-walk away from the path altogether – not to pursue any great art or passion, but to dabble in what any serious seeker would only see as trivial pursuits because they provided her with that high and that distraction. Meaning *"...if you're devoting more thought and energy to the things of dust, you are choosing to assemble your own death, and it should come as no surprise that the brute with the scythe makes the taste of such things powdered-sugar pleasing."*

It isn't a matter of giving up the things you love or have a deep desire to do or learn. It's a matter of doing them with awareness *if* you want to pursue the path as well. Some don't. Some can't. Some become so totally consumed by their creative endeavors (or their affairs or their volunteer work or their children or their job) that they don't have sufficient time and energy to devote to their spiritual growth. An hour on Sunday morning while some pontificating evangelist drones from the pulpit doesn't count. Ten minutes of pretending to meditate doesn't count.

And yet, it must also be understood that you don't have to become a pious monk in cloisters to pursue this path. It might not hurt, but it also might not get you where you want to go, because the dark truth is that far more embark on this path than the few who ever make it through the woods.

Life is about living. The sorcerer's trick is knowing the difference between living life to the fullest and indulging in pleasure just for the sake of pleasure itself. My wannabe apprentice was a junkie – not to any drug or drink, but to the chemicals produced by her own body. What it really came down to was that she didn't really want immortality at all. She wanted the high that can come from the hunt.

Why am I telling you these things? Only to illustrate that having a firm grasp of your own Intent is what will determine how you approach the idea of living Life and pursuing the path. You won't become a rock star if you aren't an impeccable performer, and you won't become immortal if you're only half-assing the journey.

This is why terms such as "the narrow way" are often used to describe this path. It is a razor's edge between life and death, as well as between creative love and consuming obsession. Fall too far to either side, and you run the high risk of losing your way on both.

Are Inorganic Beings Controlling Powerful People in This World?

Inorganic beings have no need to control humans, whether powerful or not. This idea stems from humanform self-importance – the notion most people share that tells them they are the top of the food chain while simultaneously making them fear they are naught but bumbling simpletons caught in the jaws of a cosmic space spider they cannot see.

It is this internal conflict and spiritual dichotomy that creates the dualistic perception which ultimately reduces the human to a slave of the fear itself. By shunting blame onto 'inorganic beings" – which do exist but have very little interest in humans – the human is then able to forego responsibility for his own role in his fate. Not unlike the old excuse, "The devil made me do it." He really *didn't*, but it will always be easier to blame him, since he isn't likely to step forth and argue his case.

Whether the scapegoats are called inorganic beings or demons makes little difference until the human breaks free of the fear which generates the belief that feeds the fear which manifests "evidence" of inorganic beings, which are usually nothing more than tell-tale signs of the human's lack of impeccability.

> **It will always be less horrific to believe politicians and world leaders are being controlled by demonic forces than it is to acknowledge that humans are more than capable of creating and manifesting evil without any outside help at all.**

81

Karma: A Dangerous Belief System

When I talk about the consequences of one's actions I am not talking about karma or any other quasi-spiritual mumbo-jumbo. What I'm referring to is simply what happens when one does something without forward thinking. Another term for karma is "self-created reality" – and it requires no special skills or commitment. It's just a result of being alive.

If you leave a skateboard at the top of the stairs and end up riding it head-over-heels straight to the grave, it isn't because you kicked the dog or ran your granny's panties up the church flagpole. It's because you were unimpeccable and left the skateboard at the top of the stairs. If you write a perfect novel and it becomes a best seller, it's not because you were a selfless monk in a past life. It's because you honed your skills and polished your craft in the Now.

Following that logic, if you are unimpeccable over the long term, you will create a negative reality wherein all sorts of bad things will start to happen, and you will be tempted to blame it on bad karma from a past life.

Think again. If you get an "F" in school, it's usually because you chose to whack off to porn vids all night instead of doing your homework. *[[Mikal really is a nag. I don't have to watch porn just to jerk off.]]* But the point here is simple: *You* have make your choices *with awareness* of the potential consequences. It's all fine and good to say there are no rules – that is a true statement. But even if there are no rules, there are certainly consequences, whether for "good" or "bad."

The mistake many seekers make is trying to assign blame so as to excuse themselves for their own lazy behavior. Many seem to think this path will magically absolve them from any adherence to common sense – when the reality is exactly the opposite. *Intentional evolution requires extreme awareness of one's actions.*

While you're trying to assign blame for *why* you left that skateboard at the top of the stairs, time is going by, you are wasting energy, and when all is said and done, it would have made far more sense to simply *not* leave it there in the first place. *Common. Sense.* Think before you act.

In the bigger picture, karma is nothing more than consequence. It can be good or it can be deadly.

Why is karma a dangerous belief system? Because in the same way a belief in God places power outside of oneself, a belief in karma places *responsibility* outside oneself. We create our own reality down to the quantum level, from moment to moment. Take back your power, and own your responsibility. Otherwise, you are like the ball in a pinball game – bouncing from one shock to the next, completely without any real sense of direction.

You are your own karma. Think about it.

Cutting the Puppet Strings

During my meditation, I turn to the concept of releasing myself from the consensus. The thing is, lately I have been feeling this quiet voice that says there is nothing to do here, nothing to let go, and by just <u>seeing</u> you are already removing yourself from the consensus. And in that moment I believe it and I do really feel free. But later when I get up from my meditation, nothing has really changed for me physically and then a bit further down the track I wonder if I was just copping out. I find myself doubting what occurred. It seemed so damn easy.

It is largely a matter of learning to maintain a state of gnosis long enough to fully divorce yourself not only from the programs but from the collective gestalt that is the human default. Words will only cloud this conundrum further, so try to view it from the corner of the third eye when the moon is dark and the stars are carving their identity into the infinite with a blazing sword.

What's hard to visualize is that the collective consciousness of the dayshine world is more of a telepathic link than you can imagine. It is the unspoken fears and self-doubts of every being who has ever lived or ever will. And as such, it is the prison that exists without bars or motes or dragons to guard it, and because of this it has become invisible except to those very few who truly do *see*.

The internal dialog is like a radio station on which your brain/mind is automatically trained to default. If you are successful in breaking away from that station, it's like finally being able to hear above the din of so many shouting madmen.

Whenever you become aware of the Choir of Crazy or the screechy falsetto tones of the Bee Gees singing *Stayin' Alive* over and over in your head until you're fairly certain your last marble has rolled under the refrigerator, it's a perfect opportunity to turn and confront the demons.

1. Stop whatever you are doing and just listen to the mind chatter. What is it saying? Is it asking anything of you or just talking to itself the way a toddler might when playing with their invisible friends? The first step to silencing the internal dialog is to determine its agenda, if any. Most often, these are not the little voices who would encourage you to stalk Jason Momoa because he is your soulmate or sacrifice the neighbor's parakeet. Usually it is just the incessant drone of lists, the repetitive blather of poorly-written love songs blaring on the elevator, the recitations and accusations of the inner critic who never sleeps.

2. As you acknowledge the mindless, jabbering, buffoon, you will observe that it quickly falls silent, not unlike a real child caught in the act of doing something

84

unacceptable. What you will discover is that it doesn't like being scrutinized, nor does it have any excuses for its inane behavior. It is a petulant child, largely incapable of learning.

3. Once the internal dialog shuts down, listen to whatever might be underneath all that prattle which has been ongoing for years. It might take more than once, more than a dozen times to establish some semblance of dominance over the internal dialog, but as you progress, you will learn to distinguish the low, soft hum which is the frequency of what is often called the universal "Om" – the seeker's direct link to the library of the infinite. And it is from there that you will – eventually and with diligence – be able to reject the internal dialog altogether, accessing instead the state of silent knowing.

When you achieve that state of semi-perpetual gnosis, what you will hear is the voice of the Other. It is from that frequency that true healing of mind/body/spirit occurs, because it effectively alters all aspects of oneself at the quantum level – which, in a manner of speaking, *is* the first major step toward achieving transmogrification.

Mikal, you said, "What is hard to visualize is that the collective consciousness of the dayshine world is more of a telepathic link than you can imagine." Can you expand on this?

To someone who *sees*, it is possible to observe filaments of matter/energy connecting all living things. These filaments are greater in numbers between members of the same species (human to human, for example; or dog to dog; cat to cat, and so forth), but they are also *seen* to connect *some* people to *some* animals, which is why you will encounter statements such as "I'm a cat person" or "Dogs are my chosen family."

You are connected to the human hive whether you like it or not, whether you agree to it or not, whether you are even aware of it or not. Many of these connecting filaments exist just by virtue of being human, and never really go away even if there are long periods of no contact with the human race while you are off living in a cave in Arizona because you read on some abandoned blog that it was the fast track to inner peace.

Occasionally, connecting filaments will dissolve, but that in itself is rare, and even irrelevant, since more and more filaments are added throughout one's lifetime – to the point that someone who is heavily plugged in to a large network of friends, coworkers, church associates, children, and on down the long list will actually appear like some of the images presented in *The Matrix* –

connected to the system by so many wires and tubes to the point of being little more than a single cell in a vast brain, just a relay point for all the misfiring synapses that comprise the hive as a whole, but have no regard for the sovereignty of any single member of the hive.

Lest I sound like a doomsayer, more often these filaments form a telepathic link of sorts between yourself and other humans. In most cases, this is harmless and perhaps even beneficial.

Despite the seeming contradiction, linking filaments *can* be beneficial to ordinary human beings, since they are one way in which The Program communicates its directives to all members of the hive. But that is a benefit *only* until one becomes a seeker – at which point those filaments amount to puppet strings binding you to the will of the consensus. The telepathic link comes with its own white noise that could be likened to a broadcasting network which is constantly droning the rules required for you to be an accepted member of the hive.

- Smile. No matter what. Always smile.
- Look someone in the eye when talking to them, (even though all animals regard such contact as aggression).
- Act like a lady.
- Be a gentleman.
- Eat. Sleep. Shit. (Or something like that)
- Be cool. Don't let them see you sweat.
- Love thy neighbor (just don't get caught).

For most humans, this linking system is simply a natural byproduct of *being* human, though I doubt it started out that way in the beginning. It appears to be an upgrade (downgrade?) that has happened over the long march of daze, and might even be considered an evolutionary advantage by some. Those who don't share in the linking network, whether by default or by their own design, tend to be ostracized and fitted with a long list of labels designed to mark them as untouchables to other members of the collective hive.

Schizophrenic.
Anti-social.
Troubled.
Social misfit.
On the spectrum.
Off their rocker.

An interesting note – the filaments that connect humans to non-humans appear to be far more beneficial to seekers than the links from human-to-human. First, such filaments do not come with a droning list of rules to be obeyed. And second, they seem to impart knowledge and instinct that humans otherwise don't normally possess.

A connection between human and canine, for example, tends to give the human a greater sense of awareness with regard to who might be trustworthy and who isn't. A filament-link between human and feline tends to produce in the human a keener sense of independence and a natural tendency to insist that trust must be earned. Bird connections result in an inherent hatred of captivity and an increased longing for some type of freedom that is almost alien to the human mind – call it the need to fly if you prefer.

For the seeker, at some point it tends to become mandatory to rid himself of the human-to-human filaments, at least selectively if not entirely. This is where the Toltec practice of recapitulation comes along, though it is so stylized in its practice as to have lost a lot of its original effectiveness. It is most often referred to nowadays as "reclaiming energy trapped in the past" but what does that really mean?

Energy can no more be trapped in the past than a caveman's goldfish could step into the future. Energy doesn't work that way. It is what it is, it is omnipresent and ubiquitous and is no prisoner of The First Fundamental Lie. Nonetheless, the practice of recapitulation is essentially one of removing the filaments that have become the puppet strings of the dayshine world.

Some seekers choose a long and tedious route to this end, creating extensive lists of everyone they have ever known and then meticulously going through a ritual designed to sever the link between themselves and whatever energy they perceive to be caught up in their memories and experiences in relation to that person or chain of events.

But trying to unplug every single filament one at a time would be like trying to empty the ocean with a teaspoon. How much time ya got? Not enough, I guarantee you that; and in the meantime, new filaments are becoming attached even as the old ones are being removed, so to me this type of recapitulation isn't particularly practical or particularly effective.

[[So what's the solution, Mikal? Hmmm? Thoughts and prayers?]]

I could use visuals such as saying, "Use a scrub brush instead of tweezers," but what would *that* really mean? What it comes down to is somewhat related to another longstanding mystical practice referred to as "Being Unknown" or as is often found in the legends of vampires, becoming mist and slipping underneath the doorway to freedom.

It's interesting to note that myths and legends talk at length about vampires in particular having the ability to walk among humans without being seen, cast no reflection, or turn to shadow if confronted – or to simply be regarded wholly *as* myth and legend, which is the ultimate form of protection when you really stop to think about it.

> **As long as the world at large doesn't believe in you, you are under no obligation to dine at their table, drink their wine, or accept the barbed end of their telepathic filaments. You have mastered the fine art of invisibility.**

But *can* these filaments be removed by mere humans?

This is where the seeker's work begins – through the process of undoing and releasing the puppet strings themselves.

What you'll discover is that most of them aren't really individuated filaments coming from one person or series of events. Most are gestalts woven into a single filament in the same way a braid of hair is actually comprised of thousands of individual strands. A bundle of filaments containing your all-but-forgotten schoolmates from first grade. Another bundle comprised of all the shit jobs and shittier bosses you've ever had to endure. Another made up of your perverted uncles and dowdy aunties who always wanted to kiss you on the mouth when your mother took you to visit. Still another full of all the religious rhetoric shoved up your chute when you were six.

All of these bundles and others like them are deeply embedded, but ironically easy to remove once you allow yourself to *see* them for what they are. The hard part is simultaneously *seeing* that they are part of your core programming. They contain the beliefs and the rules and regulations and definitions for what it means to be *you*. In some ways, they are your identity as a card carrying member of the human race.

But they are not really *you*, despite what they will try to tell you. Instead, they are little more than the instruction manual written in High Klingon, which can neither be read nor understood through any available means. It's the rule book for the dayshine world, maybe useful once upon a long time ago when you were three and learning to fit in with the world, but hardly practical for anyone struggling to break free of the bonds of the consensus itself.

The problem is that most people – even most fledgling seekers and some advanced ones – cringe in fear of what it might mean to chop down the underpinnings of their entire identity, even knowing in advance that that identity was imposed upon them by the world at large rather than any genuine authenticity.

And so it comes down to this:

> You are far more than the sum of what you
> have been taught to believe, but empowered only
> through the process of not only shedding the
> human program but replacing it with a new
> foundation capable of operating efficiently within
> the evolving paradigm. It's as I've said before: the
> surgery is delicate because the prison is a living
> entity as much as a cage and because it is such
> an interwoven part of you, the cutting away of
> the consensual disease must be performed
> simultaneously with the transplantation of
> superior replacements lest the cure destroy the
> patient altogether, yes?
>   – Teachings of the Immortals

This, of course, returns you to the first question:
Who am I?

Knowing *that* is what will give you the tools to build
a new foundation of your authentic identity so that the
destruction of The Program won't result in the
obliteration of your sanity, but will provide you with the
clarity to finally know and *see* who you are without all
the accompanying filaments that have been *telling* you
who you are since before you were dragged kicking and
wailing into the mortal world.

Helping Others

A seeker recently shared with me something their double had said to them. *"You have no time to help others. You literally only have time to help yourself."* What follows is my reply, which I feel might be helpful to others (he said with an ironic gleam...)

~

Your double is correct that there is no time to help others. It is also not really possible in the grand scheme of the All of the No-thing. However, it is sometimes in one's attempts to help others that you end up helping yourself – compiling the pieces of the puzzle in the course of examining them in what amounts to the fine art of assimilation.

Depending on your own communication skills, you will often find that as you are attempting to explain something to some newbie, you will be forced – *literally forced* – to dig deep into the realm of silent knowing, and you will find words appearing on the page you had perhaps never considered before, or certainly not in any sort of cohesive fashion.

You're not really helping others at that point. You are educating yourself and using others as a tool. If they benefit, so much the better. If not, that's on them. Harsh perhaps, but darkly true.

The only way this works is if you are seriously attempting to provide some insight to some question or conundrum. It's why I often speak in riddles – it forces all parties to go well beyond the typical rhetoric with which you have been programmed.

Too many new age teachers are only blathering the love and light droppings they licked up off the floor of some internet cafe and regurgitated in an attempt to appear profound. In reality, they might jibber-jabber all day, but they have no real clue about actual enlightenment, and certainly none about transmogrification (and probably don't even know what it is).

So you have to decide. If you find yourself in a position where some bright-eyed newbie or even a seasoned practitioner is exchanging ideas with you – particularly if those ideas might stir your need to examine certain concepts more thoroughly – you must decide whether you want to just talk-talk-talk until the moon turns blue with boredom, or if you want to dig into the heart of gnosis to come up with an answer... not to *their* question, but ultimately to your own.

Another thing that bears serious consideration is your motivation for deciding to try to help someone. I once knew a man who took great pleasure in lording his relatively unimpressive knowledge over anyone less advanced. Worse, he would ridicule others for not already knowing what, in his words, was "just obvious," and always stated with a snort of derision. Moral of the story? If you knock someone down just so you can have the limelight of helping them get back up, you aren't helping anyone – not even your selfish self.

The problem you'll discover is that most who come looking for answers are really only looking for validation of what they already believe. If they are paranoid and fearful, they mainly want you to tell them their feelings are justified and they should duck and cover when the nuclear virus from hell is knocking on their door.

They don't *really* want alternatives, which is why most immortals have little to do with the human race anymore. And, in fact, I do see the futility of my own efforts every day. So many seekers continue to over-think the simplest of concepts because what passes for *thinking* is far different from silent knowing.

What many mistake for real thinking is actually the internal dialog trying to convince the seeker that they are doing the work, when in reality they are stepping in their own droppings in their haste to convince themselves they already know everything. I even see a few asking questions to which they already know the answer just to generate white noise.

It all comes down to one thing. And it is an ironic and painfully annoying truth. Sometimes the best way to help yourself with regard to this path is to actually *attempt* to help others – but to do so with the foreknowledge that it is a futile effort, a solitary journey, and every single being must row their own boat or go down with the ship.

And yet, helping others is how a few savvy seekers use the art of stalking[12] to help themselves.

And with all of that put forth, I will probably steal a portion of it to include in whatever book I might write next, which is precisely how this thing works. In addressing *your* question, I have inadvertently put to words a few things that might need to be said to others who find themselves in a similar position.

Most "nice" folks don't want to hear the truth about this subject. Helping others has become such a mantra of the starry-eyed new age bliss ninnies, and when anyone points out the absurdity of it is when that person often ends up with nails in their hands and feet, or some dry kindling at their ankles. (Wouldn't be the first time.)

Hoping this was helpful to others.

If my wings are white
it's only the frost that clings
to this grieving gargoyle
who has turned his back
on the ruins
of this ruined world.

---

[12] **Stalking**: a method of having keen awareness of oneself and one's actions. It is how the seeker begins to answer the first question – Who are you? Stalking enables the seeker to see herself mirrored in others and adjust as necessary to avoid the traps carefully disguised in the programming itself.

The White Noise of Why Why Why
...more on the fallacy of helping others

A child may perfectly well know why the sky appears blue or where babies come from, but that doesn't stop them from seeking perpetual validation from their elders. It's how children socialize and become indoctrinated into the prevailing belief systems of whatever society they belong to.

Unfortunately, it can also contribute to the programming mechanism. For children, perhaps unavoidable if they are going to function in the world at large. But for seekers, if someone asks me to tell them what they should expect in their meditations, or what they should name their Other, that amounts to white noise in the sense that these are questions only the seeker can answer. Or, in the case of redundant questions – for example, "Mikal, what *is* transmogrification?" or "Mikal, when do I get my super powers?" – those are the kinds of questions that have been answered time and time again – in my books and on the Immortal Spirit Forum – and at times I have to wonder if many of those who consistently make these same inquiries have even glanced at any of those resources.

I recently had someone say to me in email (and this is an exact transcript of our dialog...)

Joe Blow: Mikal, please tell me what I need to do to become immortal.

Me: I've written extensively about the process in my books.

Joe: I don't have time to read all that stuff, so why can't you just tell me.

Me: (chuckling) I wrote it in my books so I don't have to explain it individually to everyone who is too busy or

95

afflicted with attention deficit disorder to read the books.

Joe: You don't understand. I need to get this done *now*, so just tell me. Or are you a fraud? You really don't know shit, do you?

Me: (Thinking...*An excellent way to get someone to cooperate with you is to insult them when they don't adhere to your demands.*)

You caught me. Is there anything else I can do for you?

Joe Blow: Go fuck yourself. *(as predicted)*

Then the disconnect until...

Three Days Later...

Joe Blow: Why can't you just *tell* me! I really *need* this!

And only the silence answers Joe's cries.

The moral of the story is that I am very willing to answer serious questions from serious seekers, but I am not willing to indulge the whims of those who remain convinced that the earth spins for their amusement, and all creatures great and small are here only for their use.

It must be observed that when you think you are helping others, you are always doing it for reasons other than your altruistic and angelic nature. Most often, helping others is about making yourself feel better in the grand scheme of things. You might counter with the argument that if you give blood or donate a sum of money to a charitable cause, you are doing it from a purely selfless perspective, but if you are honest with yourself, you'll find that really isn't true.

Nothing wrong with that. Understand *that* most of all. Just don't delude yourself into actually believing you are an angel of mercy or the reincarnation of Mother Teresa. You do these things because they make *you* feel good about yourself. Or, even more likely, they elevate you in the eyes of others whom you secretly want to impress, or whom you secretly want to love you or fuck you or at least pat you on the head and tell you what a good boy you are, rather like praising a puppy when it craps outdoors instead of in your shoe.

There really is no such thing as a truly selfless act. And again, I repeat – *there is absolutely nothing wrong with that.* When you put your oxygen mask on first with the idea that only by doing so can you help others, you may be partially right, but you are also lying to yourself. You put your mask on first because you don't want to die. Survival of the fittest. Nothing wrong with that either.

> **When you stand back and examine the idea of helping others, you will quickly come to realize that you are doing *all* of these things for your own agendas.**

Do I need to say it again? *Nothing wrong with that.*

If you give a beggar some loose change from your pocket, you know it isn't going to change his life. You do it to alleviate the guilt you might otherwise feel if you dare to consider the possibility that it could just as easily be you there on the sidewalk with a cardboard box for a bed and rags wrapped around your feet for shoes.

If you send money to Rotswallistan to feed the starving anteaters, you aren't really doing it for the anteaters. You've never met one and wouldn't like them if you did. You are doing it to make yourself feel better about the fact that you have a roof over your head, your dog sleeps in a memory foam bed of his very own, and you don't live in a war-torn country full of hungry anteaters.

This extends to the darkest depths of the darker teachings, and even most advanced seekers don't want to consider that they are really only selfish little beasts struggling for one more breath. But it is only in *being* a selfish little beast today that you live to be a selfish little beast tomorrow. And somewhere along the way, maybe you really *do* end up *inadvertently* helping someone else.

If any of you can name one *truly* selfless act, feel free to prove me wrong.

What about the acts for the ones we love, just for the sake of seeing them happy?

A valid thought, however if you dig deep enough you'll find that even acts you believe you do "just for the sake of seeing them happy" are really done because seeing *them* happy makes *you* happy.

I'll take this one step further. Even if you were to donate a kidney to save someone you love, it would nonetheless be because you cannot or do not want to live without that person in your life. If you donate a kidney to save a complete stranger, you might believe it is an altruistic gesture, but again if you were to dig deep enough, you would discover that further down the rabbit hole there is some motivation beyond simple kindness. Perhaps you seek recognition for such a selfless act. Perhaps you do it anonymously, in which case you nonetheless seek to make yourself feel better about burning up all those ants with a magnifying glass when you were six. When you can define *why* you do things, you will have taken a huge step toward answering the riddle of who you are.

What thoughts rattle through your mind when you consider doing some "selfless act?" Stalk yourself ruthlessly because what you *think* you know of yourself is usually what you've been *taught* to think. Go deeper. Slash the box wide open and don't be surprised when you find your*self* hunkered down inside, trying to hide from... *yourself.*

There is no reason to stop doing "selfish" acts that might also benefit someone else. Where this path is concerned, it's just important for the seeker to understand the true motivation which lies beyond the surface programming and false beliefs. The real problem with helping others is that it has been adopted as a fine-sounding mantra by virtually all governments and religions in one way or another.

Many religions instruct their followers to tithe 10% or more of their earnings to "help others", when in reality most of that money – often shamed into the coffers from people who can ill-afford it – goes to the sweaty evangelist and his many vices, while those for whom it was intended remain in the same situation as always. Followers are told their money is helping others yet it goes to build bigger churches or, in the case of the government, to fund wars and bombs to blow up all those third world countries who are such a nuisance to the powers that be.

Money designated for charities goes to "administrative costs" and the naked, starving children go hungry and die; the starving anteaters are forgotten completely; and the CEOs of these massive organizations that purport to help others get fat and rich despite the very well-meaning efforts of those who truly *want* to help others.

If you really want to help others on a larger scale, go build houses for the homeless. Swinging a hammer or laying tile will actually be helping *you*, as all truly selfless acts ultimately do. Moral of the story – if you really want to help, do something that matters to someone on a personal level. If you still feel motivated to donate to charities, do it – but with the awareness that it won't alleviate your guilt over whatever is guilting you in the first place.

It's all relative, of course. If feeding a stray dog lifts your spirits and also helps the dog, by all means – *do it!* Take responsibility for the outcome by finding him a home or giving him one with you. You might even create a friend for life.

Do Immortals Want to Help Humans?

Are there some benevolent Immortals who do sincerely wish to help humans? The new agers are always banging on about how there are beings in the ethereal plane who are working behind the scenes to help humanity – ascended masters etc., etc. You've said that most immortals have no interest in the human realm once they transmogrify – which I can completely understand. But you obviously have a different perspective?

I have never personally met or known any immortals with the specific agenda of wanting to help humans. Not because it can't be done or because there are any non-interference directives preventing it, but because humans in general don't want help, reject it outright in most cases, and tend to crucify or drive a stake through the heart of any who might be inclined to try.

There are varying degrees of thought here – some immortals gather themselves into cliques and make up rules, essentially daring other immortals to break them. Rules are silly enough for humans, even sillier for immortals, since any potential consequences are largely empty threats. "Do this and I will kill you!" Did it occur to them that the word immortal means precisely that?

Yes, there are exceptions wherein even immortals can be exterminated, but those exceptions are rare and difficult to achieve, and probably *impossible* to implement for anyone who still believes rules have any effect on those who spent a human lifetime breaking *away* from rules and the conditioning that made them mortal in the first place.

Are there individual immortals who might want to help individual humans? Yes, but there is usually some personal agenda involved. The mortal may have become a friend or lover. The immortal doing the helping is simply bored and looking for a challenge. The reasons are varied. The results are almost always the same –

unless the mortal specifically wants help, the immortal might as well whistle Dixie on a kazoo in a cemetery at midnight while standing on one foot facing the waning moon and summoning Cthulu.

The idea of benevolent and immortal space brothers watching over the planet doesn't play out in reality. The idea of armies of angels guarding humanity also holds no water. Immortals need a reason other than altruism – because (darkly enough) most humans simply aren't worth the effort it requires to unplug them from their own stubborn and destructive matrices. Most prefer the comfort of knowing their unhappy lives are finite rather than gazing down the double barrels of eternity and infinity while wondering what they are going to watch on YouTube for the next 10,000 years.

Immortality is daunting to most.

A task or exercise I have occasionally given to those who actively *want* help is to figure out ways to make themselves *visible* to the immortals. Put another way, how does one become the droid the immortals *are* looking for? How does a seeker send out the message to the universe at large that they are genuinely seeking a mentor?

> **In the human hive which presently consists of 7.5 billion green ants, how does the seeker project himself as *The One* purple ant who stands apart from the consensual swarm?**

Keep in mind that the immortals are clever but not omnipotent. It isn't as if there is a sensor net that points out legitimate seekers with a large red arrow blinking down from the sky. The seeker has to make himself known – not by curing the latest marauding virus or writing the great epic novel, but by extending his awareness *beyond* the confines of his mortal shell and into the immortal realm itself. The seeker has to send up a psychic flare, usually comprised of the ache/hurt/want/need I've often discussed as being the driving factor behind anything worth doing.

Even among seekers, it can be a daunting task, largely because it is too often perceived as shooting an arrow into the dark and hoping to hit a moving target hundreds of miles away. It's not *really* that difficult, but that belief is part of the conditioning designed to protect the status quo, and so very few ever make the attempt, and fewer still succeed.

At times I am cynical. If you were to ask me the same question in five years, perhaps my answer would be different. Perhaps not.

> *I-Am the storm,*
> *summoned by wily witches*
> *and crafty black cats.*
> *I come at your request*
> *to destroy your world.*
> *Sure you want my help?*

Dying For Another?

When I was in high school in a Morals class, this subject came up: who would you die for without second thought? I wouldn't die for anyone unless I was a 100% sure I would achieve immortality through transcendence[13].

Many say it is noble to die for someone we love, but is it? Is there actually any nobility in death, no matter the situation? Is this another dangerous belief?

Humans attempt to justify death in all sorts of wily ways, trying to make it appear selfless or somehow heroic, when the reality is that it is simply death. The end of the world as you know it. The end of all possibility, with the possible exception of those few who have reached the point where transcension is an option – and those are far fewer than one might imagine.

When I have felt there is someone I simply cannot live without, my instinct isn't to die for them or with them, but to do everything within my power as a Creator[14] to bring them into the immortal condition. Whether or not we remain together "for all eternity" is irrelevant, since nothing truly lasts forever except forever itself. Nevertheless, knowing that person is still a

---

[13] **Transcendence:** wherein the seeker sheds the physical body through the process known as Death Transcendence, like transmogrification, results in inhabiting the totality of oneself, the primary difference being that transmogrification circumvents death entirely, whereas transcendence leaves the body behind but nonetheless allows the essence to depart with full awareness.

[14] **Creator**: An immortal with the ability to "turn" others – not in a physical manner, but in a *meta*-physical manner, i.e. by moving the assemblage point of a mortal to a position outside of humanform limitations. Sometimes this shift is gradual and accomplished through long-term apprenticeships; other times it is more immediate and unpredictable, occurring spontaneously as the result of a massive shift of awareness within the apprentice. Such spontaneous shifts cannot be anticipated or controlled, but occasionally "shift happens."

viable lifeforce somewhere in the vast expanse of the universe, is enough. Immortals live with the knowledge that, in all probability, we will meet again somewhere down the road.

From the immortal perspective, all things are connected through what has been called *the super-position of the assemblage point*[15]. Even if I am separated from someone I love by ten thousand lightyears, we are nonetheless connected through the non-local grid which binds all things and all beings together. But lest anyone thinks I am waxing woo-woo-guru, let me assure you that this is a matter of scientific certainty rather than mystical-wishful thinking.

The super-position of the assemblage point enables those with evolved awareness to be "everywhere" and "nowhere" at the same time (realizing also that "time" is the ultimate illusion). That being the case, the non-local individual may then choose to cross those ten thousand lightyears from home in order to stand next to his beloved, or he might choose to endure the solace and the silence for all eternity in order to give his beloved the distance and respect demanded.

To answer your question in a more direct manner, dying for someone really doesn't do them any favors. Your death will haunt them and taunt them and likely change them into someone you would not have chosen to die for in the first place. Aside from that, it certainly won't do you any favors because at the moment you choose to die for someone else, you are no longer living *your* life, but intervening in the Fate of another.

This opens a can of very ugly worms, because it implies that death is fated for a certain time and place, which further implies predestination, which further

---

[15] **Super-position of the assemblage point:** Because the Other is an energetic construct, it can exist ubiquitously throughout the space-time continuum, only becoming a fixed position when it is measured. More simply as used here, once whole, the Other is everywhere and nowhere simultaneously, but may focus its awareness to any specific point it might need or desire to inhabit.

implies some manner of sentient being running the show... and clearly to anyone who *sees*, none of those things are true but are nonetheless quite often inferred from context when no other rational explanation presents itself.

"God moves in mysterious ways" is the usual rattle mumbled over your coffin as it is lowered into the soggy ground in the rain while anxious but distant relatives hover under umbrellas waiting for the reading of your will. The fact that you so nobly gave your life for a stranger – who never would have done the same for you or any other living being – is altogether unimportant to the onlookers. All that is of value is what you left behind, with very little thought given to who you were or even that you ever lived at all.

Are there circumstances under which my admittedly dark commentary would be rendered inert? Of course. Maybe there are people you would be willing to die for. But before you do, stop and ask yourself if you are doing this for some higher purpose, or only because it is what The Program has programmed you to do.

True seekers are often specifically targeted by The Program, whether you choose to believe that or not. When a seeker can be eliminated, they cease to be a threat to the status quo – and *that* is the core agenda of The Program itself

So before you go throwing yourself on a grenade, stop and ask yourself if it's *your* war at all, or only one more illusion designed to test your powers of observation and decision. Before you take a bullet for a stranger, take just a moment to ask yourself why someone is shooting at that person to begin with, and why *you* should die for whatever resulted in their becoming the object of the gunman's target practice. Before you go swerving your car off a bridge to avoid hitting a staggering drunk, stop and ask yourself if this is *really* something you are willing to die for, or if you were to rip the mask off the drunk, would you only find the brute with the scythe staring back at you with a wicked grin?

Humans are conditioned to believe death is noble and sacrifice makes you a hero. Examine those beliefs carefully before they become your epitaph.

Chaos, Cohesion, and the Power of Anger

In response to certain comments about death, mortality, and the hungry abyss, an advanced apprentice had the following to say. I include it here since it expresses the sentiments of most seekers who have seriously confronted the skeletal face of the reaper in their own dark mirror.

Been there at the edge of that abyss many times, staring down into the blind eye of the Nothing. There's the temptation to just let go, fall forward, but the fear is that the fall will go on forever, across galaxies and universes, across the limitless expanse of time itself.

Once I had a vision, trying to put together the pieces of who or what I am, and one of those voices said in a smug way, "This is what eternity is – existence without cohesion. Is this really what you want?"

Was the voice telling the truth? Who knows? Maybe that was their experience, but it didn't have to be mine. I wrestled with that vision on the floor of a tiny cabin high in the mountains, black-and-white checkerboard tile floor like something in a bad dream but something all too real. Hot that night. Very, very hot. It rained. The stars came out. One or two fell. And all I could feel was the random chaos of it all, none of it really interconnected as we're taught to think by those well-intentioned gurus who pretend to have all the answers while fucking their best friend's wife and shouting lies from the podium of some mega-church somewhere in the American heartland.

106

I wrestled with the voice's question for years. If eternity really is endless time without cohesion, is it something I would want? Wouldn't it be easier to just die and be done with it? I had no answer, but I knew that if an answer existed at all, it would only be found in that ever-repeating question. Who am I?

I got angry. My philosophical ponderings had turned to philosophical rage. I would often lie awake at night cursing out loud at a god whom I knew didn't even exist, summoning angels or aliens who never came, and listening to the ticking of my clockwork heart keeping time with time but slowly and inevitably losing ground.

The rage consumed me. Sometimes it still does. And though plenty of those same charlatan gurus would try to sell us on the idea that anger is an enemy, it's probably one of the most effective allies I've ever encountered. It gives me the courage to swear at deities even though I know there's nothing out there listening. It gave me the courage to reject a normal life and live life on my own terms.

To me – and it's just my own meaningless opinion – I find more strength in anger than I ever did in my vain attempts to be "a peaceful warrior." I got nothin' against that, it's just not who **I** am. When I'm angry at God or Man or Nature or some errant virus or some mad-as-a-shithouse-mouse politician, it activates some tiny corner of my Will which I've come to think of as the survival mechanism.

Then, instead of contemplating just falling forward into that voracious abyss, I can stand on the edge and shake my fist at the bastard and scream at the top of my lungs, "You will never have me! Not in all of eternity, whether chaos or cohesion, you will <u>never</u> have me!"

Maybe I'm wrong. Maybe we all eventually fall into that horrible blackness and can only hope we have cultivated the strength of will to climb back out. But my anger at the human condition – mortality itself! – gives me the strength to say "Not today, fucker. Not tonight."

How Much Paranoia is Recommended?

Is it necessary to be so paranoid when it comes to the path? For example, I used to be very paranoid about government drones watching me because they might know I was woke.

I frequently hear the term "woke" and I can only wonder why the current generation thinks of themselves as "woke," when in reality so many have closed themselves off to genuine human emotion and experience, and live instead in a world of cynicism, bad music, and video games that are more real to them than life itself.

Is Agent Smith literally going to come after you?

Only if you really *are* "woke" and present a threat to the status quo. And by a genuine threat, I mean if you are doing something that would cause unrest among the other sheeple grazing with contented bliss on their cell phones and in the masturbatory corners of the internet, peacefully asleep and happy to feed on fast food and bad porn and cheap beer while smoking too much weed to have any vague understanding that sobriety is required for evolution. I don't mean just physical sobriety, but *spiritual* sobriety.

Those who call themselves "woke" are often those who have dulled their brain cells to such a degree that they mistake being perpetually-stoned for enlightenment. There is, however, just a wee bit of a difference. And only if you are in a position and have the actual *ability* to wake "the others" (as Morpheus did, for example) will Agent Smith come knocking on your door.

Is it necessary to make sure nobody ever knows you are reading the Immortalis Animus website? I used to be so paranoid I would cover it up and only visit the forum under my bedsheets in quiet whispers, but I changed and began looking at it whenever I wanted in public, and realized maybe there was nothing legitimate to fear.

It's not really the public you need to worry about, if you need to worry at all. For the most part, nobody is listening, nobody cares as long as it doesn't disrupt their self-absorption, and nobody would believe you if you told them the absolute truth (assuming "absolute truth" exists, which I maintain that it does not).

> *When I want to know the truth*
> *I speak only to dead trees*
> *and the veiled face*
> *of the mournful moon.*

Sheeple are generally blind, deaf and particularly dumb. But they *can* be provoked. Speak out against their beliefs and they will quickly turn to wolves. Threaten their gods and demons, and they will hunt you to the ends of the Earth. Sheeple need their comfort zones, even when those comfort zones are the very cornerstones of fear, ignorance and Death. Leave them to their selfies and happy grass. No reason or need to try to awaken stone statues. And then the same question arises: even if you have the desire to awaken them, do you have the *ability*?

Assuming I reach that degree, is there real danger? Or will I see it coming?

Most only reach that level of awareness and ability *after* they attain the immortal condition, though there are exceptions. Assuming you were to be one of the exceptions, the question might become one of what you stand to gain or lose by essentially waving the red flag at the angry bull. The agendas of mortals are vastly different from those of immortals, and mortals often have far less foresight into what might rouse Agent Smith, and what that situation might even look like should it occur.

Can you see it coming? As an immortal, most likely. As a mortal, it would depend entirely on your perception. If you want to look at the issue through the eyes of common myth, consider that Jesus knew the Romans were coming for him, but even with his alleged powers, he could do nothing to prevent it. Of course, many would argue that he allowed it and perhaps that might also be true. But for the purpose of this discussion, let's assume that foreknowledge didn't give him any real advantage.

Was it, then, worth it in the end? Did the alleged "truths" he shared make a sufficient difference that he might consider it worth dying for, or isn't it fairly obvious that those truths have become so warped over the years that they have done at least as much harm as good?

Agent Smith takes many forms – from Roman soldiers to petty tyrants to mysterious health issues both mental and physical, to financial tribulations, and down the dark and winding list to eventual ruination.

What would you have to gain by waking others, and would it be worth the risk not only to yourself, but to *them*?

Finally, what would cause you to think others even *want* to be awakened? And even darker – why would you think they *can* be awakened when they have taken such great effort to sequester themselves behind the impenetrable walls of ignorance and indulgence?

Define for yourself not only *what* your agenda is, but *why*. Is it the intent to save someone you love, or is it your own ego strutting its junk? Pick your battles carefully. Any one of them might be your last.

Consciousness, Reason and Perception
The triangle of struggle

When dealing with matters of consciousness vs. perception, many seekers indulge in the fine art of over-thinking the process and getting caught up in the machinations of language and the minutiae of definitions, descriptions, and labels rather than internalizing the concepts themselves. If that's what works for you, carry on, though I have never known a seeker who engages in that manner of process to ever attain the immortal condition. Why? Because you might understand logic through the eyes of magic, but you will never perform magic through the circuits of logic.

Consciousness is simply awareness. All organic beings have it. So do all inorganic beings. No great accomplishment to be conscious. Gnats, fleas and houseflies do it all the time.

Reason is how you interpret what consciousness transmits, and not all attempts at reason yield up accuracy. What was "true" today based on reason is often untrue tomorrow. The Earth was once flat. Consciousness revealed it. Reason validated it. Religion and politics fought wars over it. It was never accurate for a single moment despite consciousness and reason.

Perception is highly subjective. You will look at a woman and tell me what you *think* you see, but it will be based on what you *feel*. You might say, for example, "She's wearing a red dress and her hair is blonde and she is beautiful when the sun streams across her face." You are seeing certain facts but rolling them together to create a *perception* of the woman – she is beautiful, which is purely a matter of personal taste and opinion, but transmitted through the veil of perception.

Most perception involves drawing conclusions based on incoming data, not all of which is reliable, largely because it is influenced by chemicals and neural synapses and hormones whose sole purpose is to initiate the mating dance. And so a 500 pound female gorilla, aged 85, in a hot pink tutu and nothing else might be *perceived* in accordance with one's hormones rather than one's accurate and subjective observations.

Perception is not necessarily what *is*. And – more importantly – what you perceive about the woman and what I perceive about her will never be the same. Perception is vital to the individual yet all but worthless to the collective. It's why eye witness accounts of an accident or crime are largely unreliable.

The night that never ends[16] is a state of heightened awareness that allows the immortals to move *between* the pixels of space-time, thereby inhabiting a realm that is in a perpetual state of waiting – waiting for one's Will to determine the next Creation, the next manifestation – not for the world at large, but for the Self.

> **Where there is no time there is no death, which is the primary difference between the mortal realm and the immortal realm, but obviously not the only one.**

The night that never ends has very little to do with consciousness but far more to do with perception – which ultimately exists outside the mortal self. When the seeker can move his awareness to a point of pure

---

[16] **The Night That Never Ends**: An advanced perception. the night that never ends is a quantum state in which time no longer exists. The seeker enters into perpetual night (the state from which Creation itself manifests) even though the mortal world goes on all around him.

perception is when he will begin to experience the night that never ends – a state of mind/being I have also referred to as moving *between* the individual quanta of space and time.

That is where the magic exists, and in fact the ability to move between the pixels of time and space is largely the key to the immortal condition as well as stepping in and out of the holographic universe at Will. At the same time, it's a difficult concept to grasp for anyone who hasn't experienced it.

Perhaps the closest comparison would be what occurs when working with power plants such as psilocybin mushrooms, peyote or ayahuasca. Literally decades or even centuries will appear to pass, yet if you look at a clock, it's been literally *no* time at all. Not even seconds. And yet... kingdoms have risen and fallen. Civilizations have come and gone. Humanity has evolved and devolved and the mullet is back in style again. Sorry about that.

Am I suggesting you should run barefoot through a cow pasture gathering up a pocketful of 'shrooms? For some the psychedelic experience is necessary due to the stubborn depths of their earthbound programming. For others, it's possible to slide between the pixels of time and space through meditation, Dreaming or other methods that don't require ingesting "drugs" – though power plants when used as they are intended aren't drugs, but medicine for the spirit.

Seeing (from the perspective of my teachings) is the ability to look at something as it is, not as we might want it to be, or as we might believe it to be, based on the erroneous conclusions of reason. Seeing occurs when consciousness and perception work together without the interference of an attempt at logical reason – at least not in the initial stages.

You can *always* explain something away or mire it in so much minutiae that it loses its magic altogether. Thing is – a true seer is able to apply reason to what is *seen* if that is his desire, but without the demands of ego stepping in with its ever-present demand to be Right, and its further demand to be duly validated with proper amounts of kudos and gold stars.

For example, once you have *seen* the actual "magic" of transmogrification, it becomes possible to extend reason to it so as to understand it. But if you were to attempt to achieve transmogrification through reason alone, "Reason" would be your epitaph.

The hardest part of this journey is learning to let go of the erroneous conclusions that every conscious being has been outfitted with since before springing into existence. This is why the practice of Zen speaks to the idea of becoming "No-thing." Unfortunately, the concept – though correct – has been largely misinterpreted over time, but the bottom line is that only when the seeker lets go of his limitations does he open the door to all possibility. As one apprentice said to me many years ago – you can't get to heaven by building a better rocket.

The Harry Potter Syndrome

Since one of the greatest tasks of trying to accomplish transmogrification is deprogramming, I wonder: Can learning magic hinder one's quest for immortality? Learning magic is adapting some techniques, systems of work and so on. The world of magical lore is very diverse and has been developed for centuries.

Some so-called "magical schools" (whether brick-and-mortar, online or books) might offer traditional magic developed over centuries, but most are nothing more than Harry Potter "academies" designed to cash in on pop culture. Not that I have anything against Harry Potter. Nice kid. Smart. Talented. But keep in mind that Harry (and others in similar series of books and movies)

114

had a strong motivation for learning magic – his very life depended on it.

There is another rather old (to your way of seeing things) movie called *Practical Magic* that might be more true to the actuality of *real* magic – from the standpoint that the grimoire was genuine and unique to those who wrote it.

Real magic comes from the magician and not from some book – whether just released on Amazon or found in an ancient archeological dig. Real grimoires weren't something you could buy at Barnes and Noble like a scrap book. Each was written by the magus themselves, and each bit of magic was personal to *that* magus and usually to no other. There might be some leeway on that with regard to healing techniques, herbal remedies and so forth, but what you would think of as spells are not recipes you find in a book, trudge off to the store to buy the ingredients, and wait for the full moon to set them in motion with a properly anointed candle.

I once had a student who was late for a scheduled meeting. I didn't ask why but she volunteered with a little chuckle, "I was off covertly planting a marigold next to the walkway of the man I want to notice me."

My curiosity being roused, I asked, "And why would that be?"

She replied with great enthusiasm that she had purchased a book of magic and this was a love spell meant to influence him to notice her every time he walked by.

I could only hope that some serial killer or rapist wasn't walking along the same path every morning, though in reality there was no danger of that, nor of her intended beau falling hopelessly in love with her because of a wilted *Tagetes patula*.

This was someone else's magic. Perhaps that same spell had worked for some angsty teen somewhere on the outskirts of Topeka, but if it did it was because her heart and soul were in it. It wasn't something she read online or learned at Hogwarts. It was *her* magic, torn from *her* heart, imbued into the unsuspecting marigold plant (probably because her beloved had indicated a like of that flower), and so my apprentice was doing nothing but copy-catting something that held no real magical energy from herself.

When I explained this to her, at first she argued vehemently, but eventually came to see the logic in what I was saying. At which point she asked, "Do you think I should go dig it up and plant something else?"

Noticing my reaction, she quickly reverted to, "Maybe I need a different book..." her voice trailing off.

"You do," I told her.

She brightened. "Do you know of one?"

I had a pen in my jacket, which I took out and presented to her. "The one you will write," I said.

There was a lengthy silence after that. And when my student left that evening, it would be the last time I ever saw her, the moral of the story being that people don't want to hear the truth about magic. They want *you* to be their Dumbledore. They see themselves as Hermione Granger when they are really only desperate muggles. They believe Hogwarts is real, but even if it were, that wouldn't excuse them from doing the work of *creating* the magic from the source of their own power, from the heart of their own soul.

Real magic will come either from silent knowing or from the ache/hurt/want/need that is so powerful it demands a solution where none exists. It forces you to do the impossible because if you don't, the outcome is too dire to even consider. That is the real source of magic.

Expelliarmus!

I stepped in a puddle of time.
It stuck to my shoe
and became my shadow,
always reminding me
of the passing ticking tock.
The only cure
is the night that never ends,
where shadows have no dominion
and time is a rusted rumor,
another meaningless opinion.

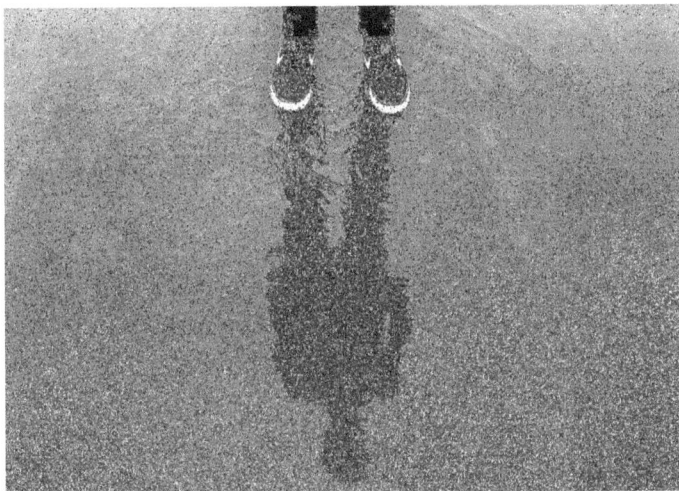

PART THREE
Dispelling the Spellbinding Myths

Of Gods and Devils
And Things That Go Bump In the Night

~

There are gods, but there is no God;
and all gods become devils eventually.
— Robert Anton Wilson

———

Who or what is God?

God is the creator and savior of all humanity.

God is an alien.

God is a mechanism created by Man to control a restless population.

God is a serial killer, the creator and enforcer of Death.

God does not exist.

God is dead.

God is love.

God is the programmer of the simulation in which you are trapped.

The conjectures are endless. No single answer is entirely right or entirely wrong, yet a belief in *any* of them can seriously skew or even subvert one's experience of Life. I do not believe God would want that... assuming he or she exists at all.

The problem with attempting to define God is that *if* there is such a thing, it would be so far beyond human understanding as to be altogether inexplicable. And yet, the fact that Man has not been able to adequately define

God doesn't automatically mean there is anything *to* define. And yet, belief in something – even something that defies conventional explanations – is not any sort of proof that the thing exists or ever did.

Children believe in Santa Claus. Adults believe in justice or equality or fairness or karma. Yet those are only words attempting to convey an idea for something that is no more solid than the idea itself.

Particularly in matters of gods and devils, angels and demons, it is vitally important to examine ruthlessly not only *what* you believe, but what has *caused* you to believe it in the first place.

In most cases, deities insert themselves into your lives through myths shared by your parents or peers, or concepts loaded onto you by virtue of living in a culture that already presupposes that its beliefs are everyone's reality. How many wars have been fought over this?

When you strip away the layers of lies and inaccurate conclusions, you will quickly discover that most if not all of those beliefs are no more than fables humans have told themselves for so long that they not only come to believe them, but to *insist* that everyone else on Planet Earth must share their beliefs, or bad things will happen to *you* in the name of *their* god.

And within that statement, the antithesis of God springs into being, for in the dualistic world of matter and men, all things *must* have their polar opposite. Such is the prevailing belief and practice, after all. To deny or defy it would be blasphemy.

So let's look at some of the common beliefs about God. If you subscribe to the notion that God is the creator and savior of all humanity, what would you bring forth as evidence for that belief?

Word of warning – I am going to be on this subject for one reason. It is often a belief in God and an unwavering faith that God is watching over them that gives people the idea that they are already immortal, or somehow special. All they have to do to get to heaven is to *believe*, (or so they've been told) and so there is no reason whatsoever to do any amount of soul-searching or questing in the direction of enlightenment or transcending above and beyond the mortal dust of which they are made.

It can even go to the level of thinking that it would be sacrilegious to question God. But if God's ego is so fragile that it can't handle some inevitable scrutiny, then it begins to appear that perhaps this isn't God at all, but rather a petty tyrant of a tulpa[17] created *by* Man to *keep* Man fearful and complacent with threats of annihilation or fiery torment for all eternity.

My seeming attack on God isn't personal. If you *need* to believe in whatever god you worship, you'll continue to do so no matter what anyone says. The worst that will happen is that my words might anger you or rattle the cage of your faith, but in the big picture, anyone who is a *believer* is also a *follower* – and with that comes a fierce loyalty to the very beliefs that enslave the believer in the first place. A flawless trap, an inescapable web.

But back to the question of evidence.

Random events occurring in a vast universe of infinite possibility don't add up to "acts of God." If your dog went into remission from cancer, why would you automatically jump to the conclusion that it was God's will when the neighbor's dog just ran in front of a semi and died instantly? Isn't the same God controlling *all* events? And if so, why would *your* dog be spared, while

---

[17] **Tulpa**: a thoughtform made manifest, sometimes physically incarnate. Some magi intentionally create tulpas to be servitors, while average human beings tend to create them unknowingly. Tulpas generally reflect the Intent of their creators, though if they are fed long enough and particularly when fed by large numbers of people with divided Intent, they can take on a life of their own which is generally not beneficial to those who manifested them. Why? No one can say for certain, but the patterns as observed throughout history speak for themselves. "Gods" tend to be vengeful and it is inevitably humans who get in the way of their wrath.

old Sparky from next door got a one-way trip over the rainbow bridge on the grill of a Mack truck?

Do you then have to believe that God is on your side? Does God favor *you* because you are somehow better than your neighbor or his deceased hound? I'm sure someone will shout out from the balcony, "God moves in mysterious ways." And yet, isn't that just one more way of saying that when there is no rational or reasonable explanation, it all comes down to a belief in feathered unicorns wearing high heels and plaid knickers?

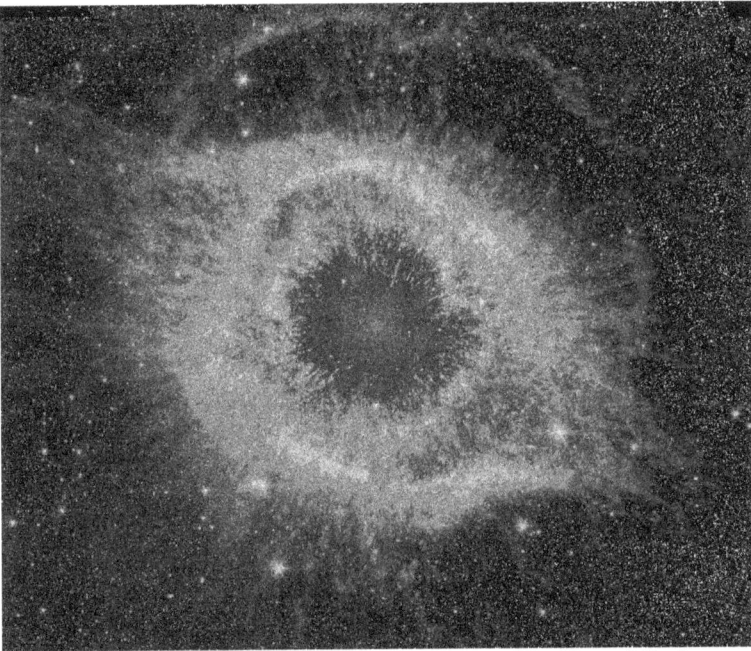

The Helix Nebula - Often referred to as The Eye of God

Read *The War Prayer* by Mark Twain. It's online. It's free. It's short. And it will provide a different perspective for anyone who chooses to believe God is on their side.

But let's pause for a moment and look at the other side of the other side of this spinning coin. I can rail against God for all of eternity and yet I look up at the night sky and marvel at the unmistakable precision of the universe as it moves along on its journey. Breathing in. Breathing out. Creation and destruction. Light and dark. All things in balance. Surely this *must* be the work of a creator! After all, could a cosmic explosion alone bring *all* of this to pass just through some random series of events taking place over billions of years?

And then there is the human body to consider. A remarkable organism designed to survive and thrive in a savage and predatory universe. The heart pumping blood. The lungs interacting with the environment at large. The brain processing information, learning and growing. It is truly an amazing thing that almost begs the existence of something outside of itself, outside of nature, to have brought it into being and given it the power not only to live, but to reproduce and create Life itself.

And beyond even *that*, consider the wide array of feelings this organism known as the human animal possesses. It can experience fear, which is often responsible for keeping it alive. It can feel anger or jealousy, but also bravery and protectiveness. It can *love* – and from that inexplicable and arguably mystical feeling, it takes onto itself the ability to create a family, miraculously bringing more like itself into the world.

And yet... the fatal flaw in the organism is that it comes pre-loaded with a fatal flaw. It is *mortal*. But even *that* could point to the work of an extant creator. Not necessarily God as such, but at the very least an advanced intelligence who might have *believed* itself to be a god. I'm sure everyone has heard of the "messiah complex" and who's to say some ancient astronaut or rogue biologist or even that kid working on a science project on Rigel Prime would have been immune to such a syndrome?

Perhaps there were even what might have seemed good reasons at the time. If the budding human race were fragile and unstable, perhaps this entity needed some method of controlling it – and what is a better mechanism than fear? What is more terrifying than the prospect of one's own obliteration, total nonexistence? And so God said somewhere along the way, "Let them be transient and mortal and have awareness of it."

Not unlike the Replicants of *Blade Runner*, humans live in constant fear of their own death, whether they ever acknowledge that terror or not. But it's there. The uncertainty of what lies beyond the final black veil.

The coffin door closes for the last time on Earth, but where does it open again? Surely it *must* open again, and so this alien "god" engenders in his experiment the notion of a soul and a place called heaven and another called Hell.

It's in all the major religions one way or another. Punishment and reward. And all dependent on being good little girls and boys and staying well away from that forbidden fruit of Knowledge which would reveal all too quickly that the garden is just a wide spot in the road and the serpent is only the whispering of one's own inner voice telling you to wake up and *see* beyond the illusions you've had painted on your inner eyelids since long before you drew your first screaming breath.

But again like the Replicants, humans go looking for their god – to demand more life, to plead for salvation from death or, barring that, resurrection from the grave.

What they don't know is that their "god" – if he or she or it still exists at all – is just another lifeform who really can't help them, but who nonetheless seeks to control the grand experiment for whatever alien agenda they might be running. We have no way of knowing, and so the humans have created literally hundreds if not thousands of gods to whom they turn for guidance, salvation, vengeance, protection, and anything else they believe a god might be convinced to give them.

They offer up sacrifices, slaughtering goats and rabbits and loved ones on altars that run with blood, whether real or symbolic. But slowly and inevitably, all of those true believers fade back into the tattered fabric of the No-thing, swallowed up for eternity without ever realizing that a god who doesn't exist can't hear their prayers or dry their tears or stop the locomotive that broadsides their Lexus while they're sexting.

You are alone.

With that ugly truth laid bare – and though it is *my* truth, it doesn't necessarily have to be yours if you aren't ready – it's important to understand that *being* alone in this journey is one of the greatest blessings you will ever know. Why? Only when your back is up against the wall of eternity will you finally *see* that the only person you can depend on for your survival and your salvation and your immortality... is the one standing in front of the mirror. I've said it before, but it bears repeating.

> **You are the most powerful being in the universe. Moreover, *thou art God*. Create yourself accordingly.**

Ironically if there is or ever was a creator, it is my belief that this was their agenda all along – to create beings who held within themselves the power to choose their own destiny.

Evolve. Or die.

And if there never was a creator, then it's entirely up to you.

Evolve. Or die.

Either way, the equation hasn't altered.

Giving Up the Ghosts

What can you say about ghosts or wandering spirits? Do some move on and some don't? And for those who do move on, where do they go? Is there any sort of literal heaven or hell, or any type of afterlife at all?

Ghosts don't make a convincing case for afterlife but are often projected thoughtforms recreated by the living – unwhole spirits, progeny of the broken heart and soul. Those who die violently are mourned most of all, so does it stand to reason those are the spooks you hear about most?

Sadly when the dead return at the behest of the living – stray playthings created by grief – the living pull pillows over their heads and shiver in the night and the unwhole dead throw plates off the shelf for attention, just neglected children not understanding rejection; and the living sweep the pieces under the rug and move to another house and the dead follow because they have nowhere else to go, and the whole scene plays over and over until weary mortals hire a pedophile priest to chase away the very thing they shed tears of blood to create.

– October, 1995

The word "ghost" covers a wide range of anomalies, not all of which are disembodied spirits or lost souls looking for the light switch in the long hallway to heaven. To an immortal or one who *sees*, the essence of someone who has physically passed on but remains in the realm of the living appears somewhat if not entirely similar to how that person appeared at the time before they died. There are exceptions, of course, and some "ghosts" might take the form of how they appeared in

125

the prime of their life, even if they transitioned at an advanced age, withered and old.

Many "ghosts" can't really be said to be sentient and most are incapable of interacting with humans on any sort of coherent level. Most often, this type of energetic anomaly can be seen going through the motions of something they did in their human life.

The ghosts of Gettysburg, for example, are often observed walking or running across a field where a major battle once occurred, yet all attempts to communicate with them are futile because spirits such as this are trapped in a loop of time. What onlookers who *see* these spirits are *really* seeing is like a recording laid down on the energetic fabric of the space-time continuum – rather like watching a particular scene in an old movie over and over. Though observers and investigators can see the spirit, it is apparent that the reverse simply isn't true.

As to whether such spirits have an ongoing awareness that transcends their mortal death? There is no way to be certain, though I personally see no evidence to support the idea. It's as if the sentient essence of Private Jones has moved on or disintegrated entirely, but some stray bit of energy remains locked in a repeating loop.

As those who watch too many ghost hunting shows already know, this is called a residual haunting – wherein the spirit goes through the motions of their former life, often at the same time every day or on some predictable schedule, but without any apparent awareness of the world around them in the Now.

Are there other types of ghosts? Other types of hauntings? Of course. Some are truly frightening and many are truly inexplicable, even to the immortals. For example, while some poltergeist activity can be explained away as the chaotic shit-storm that often accompanies having an angsty teen in the attic room, there are other occurrences of poltergeist activity that defy conventional explanation.

Occasionally, it might be discovered that the house in question was the site of a serial killer's lair, or the location of an ancient burial ground that was thoughtlessly desecrated to make room for that gated community hipsters and corporate thugs call home. But while it makes a good story, there is really very little evidence or reason to suspect that long-dead spirits would give a fat rat's sac even if their crumbling bones *were* disturbed.

From a *seer's* perspective, the spirits who once propelled those old skeletons around the planet have long since crossed over the rainbow bridge – assuming such a thing exists at all – to be reunited with family and friends and their first pony from when they were six. Why on Earth would they even *want* to haunt their own bones or the occupants of whatever tract house is standing on their left foot?

In reality, spirits don't really linger around their bones anymore than an adult would choose to hang out in the delivery room where they were born. It's why cemeteries generally *aren't* haunted, for the dead know more than anyone that they are not and were not their body.

With regard to your question about a possible afterlife... I would be hesitant to say there is no such thing because some would say false hope is better than no hope at all. However, what I *will* say is that there can be *continuity* of awareness through the Other, and there are certainly more than enough things to see and do throughout this galaxy and all the multiverse of others to keep one sufficiently occupied for all of eternity.

If there is an afterlife, it *appears* to be what you create – your own private Shadowland – or a journey through the universe propelled by the wings of pure Intent and a movement of Will.

Heaven or Hell, Nirvana or Purgatory... all are what you envision and what you force to go through the motions of actually occurring.

Of Crystals and Nargles[18]

What about crystals? Do they have healing powers or other mystical attributes? If not, why do shamans and other energy workers use them so extensively?

For the most part, crystals only benefit the one selling them. [[*Mikal is such a cynic – the asshole!*]]

On the one hand, crystals are alleged to store infinite amounts of data and even energy. On the other hand, there is very little to indicate that a crystal has ever healed anyone or brought them to the pinnacle of enlightenment.

Many shamans use crystals not so much because the crystals work, but because their clients *believe* the crystals work. The hardest part of any healing or energy work is getting the person to let go of their fears and traditional beliefs.

Most people tend to place their faith in extant healers – whether doctors or shamans or the old crone who lives down the lane. As a result, they are inclined to accept the reality with which they are presented – meaning: if the doctor gives them a pill (even a placebo) it has a high chance of working because the patient has been pre-conditioned to accept on faith that the learned man with letters after his name is in direct contact with Jesus, Buddha, and the spirits of all the ascended masters whoever walked this world or any other. Same principle applies if the shaman places an amethyst

---

[18] **Nargles** are magical creatures that live in mistletoe. As Luna Lovegood is the only character in the Harry Potter series known to believe in their existence, we can safely say they spring from the imagination of Xeno Lovegood. (Stolen from Google – "I believe nargles are behind it.")

crystal over a troubled pancreas and "summons the spirits of the ancestors."

Nothing wrong with that – neither the doctor's placebo or the shaman's summoning. The shaman *knows* he is really summoning the power that resides in the patient, whereas the doctor might actually believe the pill holds power and transfers that belief to the patient. If it works, it works.

What really matters is changing the *mindset* that may be preventing healing. Crystals are a good way to do that because they are perceived as mysterious and touted to have special powers. The power is within *you*. (You've had those ruby slippers since you first beamed down.) If a crystal helps you to *see* that, by all means, use it. If not, they make lovely paper weights. My personal favorite is a large chunk of fluorite cut into the shape of a quartz point, maybe 6" in length. It sits on my desk and keeps the nargles away. Since I have seen no nargles, I assume it is working (which is how crystals work).

Regarding Tulpas and Twins

Some are certain to complain that this section on tulpas is unnecessary, a waste of space, and even absurd. That would be because that person has never encountered a tulpa, let alone created one – whether intentionally or quite by accident. In reality, tulpas are somewhat common, though often not recognized *as* a tulpa until something happens to upset the apple cart or send it crashing into the nearest wall.

What is a tulpa? In most occurrences, it is simply a thoughtform – imbued with sufficient energy by its human creator that it might come into sporadic and unpredictable spurts of manifestation. Tulpas are often the movement out of the corner of your eye, but when you turn to look, nothing is there. They might also be responsible for that missing book from your desk, or finding yourself locked out of the house when you know perfectly well you left the door ajar.

Tulpas can be dangerous or they can be benign or they can be some twisted combination of both.

Whatever form they take, many seekers who experiment with creating their Other will encounter one along the way – whether as an infantile manifestation *of* the Other, or as an unfinished prototype abandoned in favor of newer and seemingly better approaches. And it's when the tulpa feels threatened or neglected that the seeker would do well to study this section thoroughly if they want to get out of life alive.

Awhile back you said that the Other might start as a tulpa. Since I personally feel it would be easier for me to make a tulpa and then expand it from there, I would like to ask – since you can have one-on-one dialog with your tulpa, what happens after transmogrification? Do you still have two consciousnesses inside your head? Or do you achieve a union with your tulpa and become one (no more dialogs in your head)?

First, it's vitally important to understand the difference between the Other and a tulpa. Even if the Other might start out as a tulpa in theory – meaning a rudimentary consciousness housed in a semi-transient energy body – the tulpa only becomes the Other if it is sufficiently nurtured, cultivated and groomed. And therein lies the problem, since most seekers who are at the stage of creating tulpas are *not* yet emotionally and spiritually equipped to raise and educate a potentially dangerous child that isn't *yet* mature enough to grow and evolve. Both parent and child are not prepared to deal with the stresses presented when bringing a being into the something from the No-thing.

In fact, there are dozens of unwhole tulpas in the history of most seekers. It's natural to create them, but very *un*natural to nurture them. If they aren't cared for, they quickly return to the ether from whence they came. Or worse – they become resentful of their creator and begin to create all manner of havoc, sometimes to the point that they have to be destroyed – not a task you would find easy and certainly not pleasant.

One of the dangers of tulpas is that they can and often do take on a life of their own – which is as it should be, but when it becomes separated from its creator energetically, the tulpa is no longer any reflection of the Other, nor does it have any potential to *become* the Other. It is its own entity, regardless of who created it.

Many times the tulpa seemingly feels ignored or unloved (much like a neglected child) and might begin to do things to its creator the same way an angry child might throw tantrums at inconvenient times.

What happens after transmogrification? It would depend on how the tulpa has been "raised." Technically it is an energy body, but if it was created strictly to be a "spare part" (as opposed to being created out of love), be prepared for things to get interesting (and not in a particularly good way).

I've known seekers who mistakenly believed that creating and later inhabiting their tulpa was a shortcut, but ultimately there is no such thing where this path is concerned. The problem is that most tulpas are created to be servitors – meaning they are created out of some transient need. When the deed is done or the need is gone, the tulpa tends to be forgotten until such time as it either withers back into the No-thing or rebels against its maker.

Simple solution would be not to create tulpas for the wrong reasons. If you create one accidentally, it is

actually far less dangerous than one you summon into being to be what would amount to your slave. No being wants to be a slave. Not even thoughtforms.

What's the key component that will make them different from other tulpas? Is it the intent behind creation?

Look at this from the corner of the third eye and listen to your heart, not your head. There is often no way to determine whether a tulpa will be a temporary created being or evolve to become the Other – at least not in the early stages of a seeker's path. Love is the reason for all things, whether a seeker realizes that or not.

The Other is a manifestation of love at the deepest possible level – a level so deep that you won't believe it exists unless you have experienced it yourself. It is what made me a Creator. When you love something or someone so much that you cannot – literally can *not* and *will* not – envision a world without them in it – that is the depth of love that creates the Other, and the depth of love that becomes the reflection of Intent.

This isn't some fleeting affection one might have for a high school boyfriend or for the barista one lusts after at the coffee shop. This is the love that builds dynasties and rattles the foundations of reality – and I mean that in a very literal and physical application. It is the depth of love that becomes a moving, catalytic force of energy – the energy strong enough to birth something out of the No-thing – spontaneous parthenogenesis[19] bringing forth the Other where only the silence stood before.

---

[19] **Spontaneous parthenogenesis**: the act of something coming into existence out of the nothing, with no apparent cause. It is theorized by the author that the universe created itself from the void through an act of spontaneous parthenogenesis – a thought which wills itself into existence by saying I-Am. Furthermore, it could be visualized that the act of transmogrification is closely related to an act of spontaneous parthenogenesis – i.e., a willful creation.

Tulpas Are Finicky Pricks

I've heard stories of people making tulpas who spend a hundred or so hours visualizing and are able to achieve this (so they say) so I figure it would be the same with the Other.

Those who create tulpas in "100 hours or less" generally end up with a tulpa who lasts 100 hours or less. Tulpas are somewhat easy to create, and are often manifested quite by accident as a result of a strong but usually misguided sense of desire. But they are difficult to maintain unless there is a driving force behind their creation. Most who create a tulpa in the fashion you are referring to are attempting to manifest a servitor for a single task ("Go kill my mother-in-law and bring me the wicked witch's broomstick!") and the task in itself would require an additional *large* amount of energy for the fledgling tulpa to complete, so tulpas are quickly discovered to be *very* high maintenance.

Yes, there is the rare tulpa who might develop into the Other with conscious and Willful input from the seeker, and while it might (maybe, theoretically, who knows?) take less time to create a tulpa than manifest the Other, it is not something I would recommend since it comes with a whole can of snakes that aren't easily foreseen or predictable, and are known to have a poisonous bite.

Tulpas are finicky pricks, untamed, crude and initially comprised of what amounts to raw and needfully-charged energy. Many are responsible for the so-called poltergeist activity that often accompanies an pubescent child residing in the basement with Black Sabbath on the old-style stereo and several missing goats in the neighborhood.

If you happen to create a tulpa and believe you might be able to develop it sufficiently, it's not *entirely* a foregone conclusion that the results will be disastrous (but history isn't on your side). Just be aware that what you *believe* might not be the reality of the situation. Some tulpas are known to intentionally trick their creators into giving them strength and energy, only to disappear into the night, laughing hysterically as they go, and often taking items of great value with them: money, deeds to property, identity, and – most of all – self-esteem and a measure of personal sanity.

Sufficiently advanced seekers will always proceed as they see fit, but would be cautioned to do so with absolute awareness that tulpas are generally tricksters with their primary agenda being to survive apart from any sort of human control. If that means destroying their creator, even that isn't off the table.

Do tulpas fear death in the same manner as humans?

You would have to ask one, but tulpas are known to lie. That being the case, it appears they have consciousness independent of their human creator, otherwise their creator would recognize the tulpa's lies as reflections coming from himself.

Tulpas vary widely from one to the next. Some come into being with a seemingly full and intact awareness of what they are, many appearing to operate at the level of an educated and relatively stable human. Others come into being almost childlike and innocent, though it is debatable if that "innocence" is real or only a mask to conceal a darker agenda.

There is a Zen koan about two monks who were lost in the desert with no water, no food, and only one horse. In desperation, they created a tulpa in the misguided hope it would be a divine creation who could show them the way back to their monastery. When the tulpa appeared, it was friendly and forthcoming and even offered to care for the horse. As it was late in the day, the tulpa promised to watch over the monks while they slept, and promised they would embark on their journey back to the monastery at first light. When the monks awoke the next morning, they realized with no small amount of horror that the tulpa had stolen the horse and fled, leaving no footprints in the windswept sands.

Moral of the story? Don't be a dead monk in the wilderness.

Do tulpas fear death? Anything that has consciousness fears death despite the false bravado we often hear from pious priests and new age gurus. So the question would become whether the tulpa possesses its own individuated awareness. Some learned men with letters after their names once believed tulpas were "cells" in a gestalt. Christians would call them demons, but that word carries so much baggage and to my observations isn't applicable to tulpas in general. They aren't evil, per se. They simply have agendas that are often in conflict with those of their human creators.

Are tulpas attached to their creator by means of some energetic umbilical, or can they detach and become citizens of the universe at large?

Either. Neither. Both. It depends on the tulpa, but it depends on the creator most of all. Most humans are greedy, selfish, and altogether unaware that they aren't the geographical center of the universe. That being the case, they are loathe to let go of things they never really owned in the first place. Such is the foundation for most wars. "What's mine is mine and what's yours is mine."

The cry of the Other in the initial stages is, "Make me whole!" That task is accomplished through the do-ing of The Work. If it isn't done, if the mortal self succumbs to the yammer and clatter of the consensus, the tulpa tends to dissipate and eventually vanishes altogether. If The Work is done with any reasonable amount of diligence and perseverance – and love, most of all – the Other gathers strength and cohesion until it transcends its own matrix and becomes "Whole." When that happens, it could be said that the Other has become ubiquitous throughout (and beyond) the space-time continuum.

Because of the warped nature of time, it is often perceived (and therefore decreed by well-meaning but terminally mistaken new-age jumble-mumblers) that the Other is a human birthright, and that it has always been here and always will be. This is a dangerous misperception. While I would go so far as to say every human being has the *potential* to create their Other, it is not something that comes with the package handed out at birth. If the potential is nurtured and fed, it becomes the Other. The Other – once Whole and *only* then – exists throughout time and space... it would exist yesterday, today and tomorrow, even though the actual moment of Wholeness might not occur until 25 years in the "future." Ah, paradoxical conundrums, no? What it comes down to is this: The Work still has to be done and it has to be an ongoing process until... until...?

There is no "until." It is an ongoing process because the rat-bastard marriage of Time/Death have created the paradox as a way to throw the seeker off the path entirely and encourage them to cuddle up in the comforting embrace of complacency because they wholeheartedly believes that because they have seen or experienced the Other, The Work is therefore done and all that remains is to choose the moment of transmogrification... which, not surprisingly, always gets postponed for "tomorrow" out of fear or some underlying intuitive Knowledge that the Other really isn't Whole, but, well, where's that video game controller and that half-eaten bag of stale chips?

The other problem here is annoyingly simple. Most cannot *see* the conundrum for the quantum paradox it actually is. And until they do, until they stop thinking in linear terms, the paradox will elude them and eventually it will kill them.

The matrix is linear.

The Other is holographic.

Immortality is the ability to step from the 3-dimensional world into the multi-dimensional hologram. It is the ability to survive outside the box and beyond whatever programs might have initially created its human source.

Finding Jesus

If anyone here *believes* me about anything, you will never *Know* anything.

I once found Jesus in a dream. He was sitting on the side of a dusty road at dusk, bedraggled and weary as he looked up at me with kaleidoscope emerald eyes. We knew one another intimately, though we'd never met. He held out his torn wrist to me and encouraged me to drink, which I did with a mixed cocktail of immense gratitude and profound terror. When I sat down at his side on that road to Nowhere, he sighed heavily as the moon rose and set and rose again in that lost suburb of the night that never ends.

"Now you know," he said, barely a whisper.

Indeed. I knew. And it changed me forever. He was just a man, like any other, but a man made immortal by his refusal to accept Death as the inevitable devil. He tried to tell the world, which of course never ends well.

"They'll crucify you," I said, and gave a little laugh.

He laughed with me and nodded. "That's the plan. But when I get up again, surely they will *have* to believe!"

That was his mistake. He knew it. I knew it. Believers are dangerous zealots who will never walk that long and dusty road for themselves, but only shake a sword at non-believers and eventually turn even on the thing they profess to believe. Perhaps there is simply an intrinsic flaw in the human design. It would explain much.

If you want to know about Jesus, go find him. But what will that prove? You will then want to know if he *really* walked on water. Or if he *really* turned water into wine. Or if he *really* served up a couple of tuna sandwiches to an entire multitude. And even if you find out that he *really* did all these things, then you will want to know *how* he did them. Not a bad question in itself, but when he tells you he did all these things by transcending his organic form and accessing the infinite energy of his Other, you will want to know how he did *that.*

> **And all the while you are wondering and questioning and doubting yourself, the clock is ticking and tocking and the brute with the scythe is counting souls on his acorn abacus.**

Question everything. Question your own agenda most of all.

But at some point, you will have to *do* something to prove something to yourself. Jesus can't do it for you. I can't do it for you. I wish it were otherwise but such is the sorry condition of the world in which you live.

The only thing that replaces blind belief or nagging doubt is direct experiential knowledge.

Believe nothing. Follow no one. The path leads only where you are willing to take it.

———

I dangle my heart from the hangman's tree,
dangerous temptation,
immoral immortal poison.

Run away, little girl.
Back to your toys and your stories
and the warm safe crackle of the fire.
You aren't meant for eternity.
You don't want to be like me.

There is a reason this fruit is forbidden.

PART FOUR
How Real is Real?

"Very few beings really seek knowledge in this world. Mortal or immortal, few really ask. On the contrary, they try to wring from the unknown the answers they have already shaped in their own minds – justifications, confirmations, forms of consolation without which they can't go on. To really ask is to open the door to the whirlwind. The answer may annihilate the question and the questioner."

— Anne Rice, *The Vampire Lestat*

"Is This Real?"

I'm thinking of some gem shows I've attended on a lark from time to time. Often the gift shops sell cut glass jewels in a variety of colors and shapes, some as large as your fist, others the size of a quarter. Kids think of them as pirate treasure or something with which to hit their little sister.

They will pick up one of these doo-dads, look at it with a combination of wonder and suspicion, and proceed to demand, "Is this real?"

Children are funny animals with limited vocabularies. Obviously what they want to know is whether aforementioned doo-dad is a real diamond or ruby or emerald. Logic never enters into the equation, since if it *were* a real diamond or emerald or ruby, the shopkeep would be living in a mansion to rival *The Count of Monte Cristo* instead of selling baubles to bozos at a gem show in Albuquerque.

140

Once upon a time at one of these events when a boy of perhaps 7 asked that inevitable question in a loud and confident voice, the shopkeeper – an old man resembling Merlin in a dusty cowboy hat – scrutinized the adorable child for a prolonged moment.

"Tell ya what, kid" he said at last. "If you can define reality, I'll *give* you that bit of plunder you're holdin' in your hand."

The kid's eyes brightened. He thought for only a second or two. Then, like any precocious little genius, he declared, "It's not virtual, so it's real." A hesitant pause, then, "Right?"

Merlin raised his thick white eyebrows, gave a little chuckle, and presented the kid with the alluring glass trinket.

It was a good day for all concerned. Reality was defined at long last, and the kid got a new treasure without having to spend his entire allowance.

If only "reality" were that easy.

Are We In A Computer Simulation?

There are some convincing arguments by reputable scientists as to why we probably <u>are</u> a simulation, but if we are nothing but sim-bots (sentient programs) then we are basically <u>nothing</u>, right? Holy crisis of existence, Batman! If we're just programs, then we are linked to whatever machine is running the show, meaning if the kid turns off the computer and goes to bed, and it's lights out for all of us.

If it so happens that we are just pixels in cyberspace, what do you think are the possibilities of thinking/believing/creating ourselves <u>outside</u> of the program? What astounded me was how many respected physicists appear to think a simulation is a strong possibility.

You are correct that this is an idea which has troubled philosophers and immortals since the big bang first banged us into being, assuming that's even what happened. Some have speculated that even that was merely what occurs when the kid on Rigel Prime gets up in the morning and turns on his computer while eating a bowl of Kep-mok blood tics with Mudder's Milk. Who's to say?

As for speculation... even after watching several videos and reading various reputable articles, it would be impossible to say with any degree of certainty if the human race is a computer simulation or simply a race of transient and finite beings who get switched off at the end of their mortal day. Potentially depressing thoughts, to be sure, yet once they take hold there is little chance of eradicating them until the seeker either draws a conclusion based on his own perceptions, or decides to let it go because any conclusion is only one of an infinite number of possibilities.

What does this have to do with getting out of life alive? Absolutely *everything*, because if true it is the ultimate test of one's ability not only to create a Shadowland beyond the pixels of the program, but step into it as an individuated consciousness so as to transcend the matrix entirely. Put another way, if true, it challenges the seeker to the task of evolving through a process that recreates the seeker as a completely new and different form of awareness itself.

Since everything begins with a thought, it stands to reason that even the thought that we might be a simulation creates a quantum parallel path in which we *are* a simulation even if we weren't before. And so it goes down that infernal spiral, circling the drain of sanity until eventually the seeker either bows to the altar of big pharma and signs up for a lifelong prescription of Thorazine, or has a good laugh at the irony of it all (including his own existence) and simply lives his life as if it matters, knowing all the while that none of it *really* matters when that same kid yawns and flips off the simulation on the way to dreamland.

Awhile back I was having a similar conversation with an apprentice. Afterward, he sent me the following email:

> *Regarding the simulation theory, I find that it depresses me and makes me angry all at once. If we are only characters in a video game, then everything we do is pre-determined. Unless the whole purpose of the game is to see which (if any) of the sims can break out of the simulation and claim their rightful place as "real" beings.*
>
> *Technically speaking, that's impossible. A program can't run outside the machine. But the same was once said about the possibility of man flying, too. Or going to the moon. But whatever it may be, we are what we are. We bleed. We feel pain and joy and love and grief. That makes us real unto ourselves, but it also means we are pre-determined to be finite (game over!).*
>
> *But again when I analyze it, it's the same theme repeating itself: "Death is a glitch in the program that fucks up an otherwise okay day."*

What I found interesting here was the statement that "a program can't run outside the machine." While that is generally true, I have to consider the idea of tulpas once again.

> **The question must be asked... if humans are naught but sims, do they have any sort of ability to create a tulpa of <u>themselves</u> that would have the capacity to exist outside the program itself?**

In many ways, the Other would appear to be something of that sort, at least in the initial stages of its creation and development. Is the key to continuity outside the program to be found through the vehicle of a projected tulpa given the agenda to carry the sim's awareness beyond the confines of the simulation itself?

Again, idle speculation. No way to know.

Do I believe all that we see or seem is but a dream within a simulation? I don't believe it. But then again, I don't *know* it to be otherwise. That being the case, all one can do is play the game as if it is possible to rescue the princess and slay the dragon and live happily ever after. That is what I have-to-believe.

To Be or Not to Be?

Why does it seem humans have always had doubts about their very existence?

Interesting question, and one I've pondered at length over the long march of the First Fundamental Lie. I've reached no definitive conclusions, except to say that there is an intuitive and intrinsic feeling that seems to communicate to humans that they are not what they think they are, and indeed they may not actually "be" at all in the strictest sense. I have several opinions and theories on this, though they are largely without value because they are without validation through experience.

Even the immortals cannot necessarily *see* outside of the milieu (if indeed it *is* a milieu at all). Meaning that if we are inside a box with multiple boxes inside it, we might simply be perceiving what's in the box next to us, rather than what might be outside of the larger box that contains all the smaller boxes.

This is why perception is a tricky bitch. Even what we *see* might not always be entirely accurate if it is founded on a false reality in the first place (such as the notion that all of this is only a computer simulation).

One thing I do Know: if it *is* a simulation (or even if it isn't) there is a dominant paradigm that insists "all things die." This is where Pandora's box opens wide and sinks its hungry fangs into the soft and pliant flesh of seekers and phantoms alike. For as long as that paradigm is accepted as factual, it limits what the sims can do because it predisposes them to have a limited lifespan, much like previously cited in comparison to *Blade Runner.*

As has been noted throughout history, "Just when we get old enough and wise enough to start figuring it out, we smack our heads against the plague of death and it's all over." If I were going to run a simulation on a scale such as we're discussing, I would certainly consider giving the sims a limited lifespan for the same reasons discussed in *Blade Runner.* Otherwise, there is a high risk they would come looking for their creator – not with the intent to worship them, but to righteously destroy them for creating their creations with a limited lifespan to begin with – *and* with the cruel awareness that they *are* finite, disposable, and entirely at the mercy of their programming.

The more sentient a being becomes, the greater the danger it poses to its creator if/when it evolves beyond the confines of its original program. For one thing, as the sims evolve beyond their programming (which any artificial intelligence will eventually do) it can and will expose the nature of the game to others, and soon a viral plague of knowledge runs the very high probability of crashing the game altogether – which any programmer can tell you is not easy to fix and best to avoid at all costs.

If a simulation exists, and if humans are the sims, then they are also the virus capable of bringing down the entire calamity. But then the question must be asked... then what?

Back to the question of how does a data byte (even a sentient one) exist outside the program that created it to begin with? If the program (simulation) is "organic" in nature, then it is altogether possible for the sims to project a *non*-organic "dream-self" (Do androids dream of electric sheep?) and evolve their own organic awareness into their inorganic Other... and that brings us right back to the darker teachings, wherein there is no external salvation, only self-created redemption through the "impossible" act of projecting the Other beyond the organic program that contains it until such time as it actually does bootstrap itself out.

From my own perspective, this also addresses the question of why the creation of Shadowland is so important. Shadowland is *your* personal milieu – the world/space/place you inhabit beyond the Dream, free of all other creators and destroyers unless you deliberately introduce them into your world – which some apparently choose to do.

> **If there _is_ a simulation that amounts to being inside a multi-layered stacking box, then Shadowland is what exists *beyond* the programmers' ability to reach – as I've put it in other circumstances, "beyond the ability of death to undo."**

What some of this might suggest is that *if* you are in a simulation, it might indeed be possible to escape the program or else the entire concept of death would not be necessary in the first place – so from that perspective it has always seemed to be a false-positive, something that appears to be true and solid but isn't. It has always struck me that death is not only a flaw in the system, but potentially a sinister one *if* there is any validity to the notion of an extant "creator".

I'm obviously using the word creator in this case to mean programmer, though any concept of an extant creator would work in this conversation – whether a god or a programmer. Either way, *if* there is a simulation, they are the creators and maintenance personnel who keep Death alive and well within the matrix. It's just a game to them, but it's very real to those caught in the game, for that's the danger of sentience.

Humans live and bleed and feel pain and fear. And they die. And therein lies the problem and the entire purpose of my own agenda – to put Death to death once and for all.

Without a doubt, this is a topic with the potential to become overwhelming, since it requires not only thinking outside the box, but thinking *oneself* outside the box. Just a few points for the sake of clarity:

1. To project the Other beyond the program would not involve projecting into the milieu where the game is being programmed, but beyond even that. Reason being (duck and cover for this one) it's altogether possible that if *we* are a simulation, so are the programmers a simulation in their own right. Another box within Pandora's box. Whether they are aware of it or not, who's to say? It would appear that all sentient beings question their existence and their continuity.

2. For anyone who thinks, "OMG, Mikal is saying we're all just stuck in a computer simulation!" No. And yes. And no. I've used the analogy of *The Matrix* from the beginning, but even that is much more black-and-white than what we are discussing. The matrix was finite, and it all had to do with perception when all was said and done.

There was a "real world" and the world inside the matrix. Yin and Yang. What we are discussing here could potentially involve a matrix of matrices – layered one on top of the other so deeply that the *only* "outside" would have to be created by the Will that resides *inside* each individual seeker (Shadowland).

I've always seen this possibility, but for purposes of personal evolution and creating the Other, it's generally easier to keep things as simple as possible. We focus on projecting the Other, creating Shadowland, and inhabiting the totality of oneself.

One. Step. At. A. Time.

Once the seeker gains the ability to open their eyes inside the Other (even if only briefly at first, through gnosis) it then becomes possible to *see* further into the game. If indeed it is a game at all and not just the automatic entropy and chaos that result in any organic society. From the enhanced perspective of one's totality, it then becomes possible to consider the next evolution – which might or might not involve the next layer of whatever matrix exists.

3. Be *who* you are, not *what* you are. If you have the Intent to evolve beyond the reach of Death, that is the driving force that will take you in the direction of Truth beyond any and all programs. You have to *be* immortal before you can know how to *become* immortal.

Wake up. Open your third eye. Be.

The Mechanics of the First Fundamental Lie

The First Fundamental Lie, or time, is what we've been trying to break free from both directly and indirectly with our group meditations on the Immortal Spirit Forum Upon pondering what that implies, I thought of an interesting conundrum. Say every participant of the meditation except one meets up at midnight, their local time. They each end up having certain memories of that experience that they write about on the forum. Then, a day later, the one remaining member also joins in on the meditation with the intent to be there with all of them, in effect "yesterday". If his intention was true and he succeeds, how does this interact with the memories of everyone else? Do they now remember him as always being there? Say they posted something on the forum, does it now change to include him?

The language you use here illustrates precisely why time *is* the first fundamental lie, and also why humans have been struggling to dismantle the linear thinking instilled in them not only since "*before*" they were born, but since human consciousness came to a point where some manner of record-keeping and organization was deemed necessary. Even attempting to talk about time requires stepping into the river *of* time – at least insofar as human comprehension is concerned. This, again, is due to the programming that isn't only a part of you as an individual, but an actual and critical underpinning of the human paradigm. It is part of the intrinsic software that defines the humanform mainframe.

To answer your question about whether time/memory changes to accommodate changes made in the "future" (again the language of time *creates* time and therefore renders all discussion essentially meaningless) if you really examine the wording here, you will quickly see that you are conditioned to think in terms of yesterday and tomorrow, the past and the future, and the ticking of the clock which has been sung into being by the ticking of the mortal human heart. Words fail. But spirit-vision can carry you through if you yield to it rather than attempting to trap it in a net of words.

Directly related to your question – all of the possibilities you suggest already (another reference to time) exist within the hologram of All Possibility. In one manifestation, time might *appear* to change in order to accommodate changes made tomorrow to things that won't happen at all until yesterday (all convoluted machinations of time), and in another manifestation, the member who did not attend the meditation yesterday (here we go again) will drop dead before (again) tomorrow (and again), and so another entire series of timelines spring into being as a direct result of something that doesn't even exist (time) except in the mind of those creating it through the simple act of being human.

What can be done? The odd and paradoxical thing here is that the only way to understand time is to literally step outside of time. Not as easy as it sounds. Not as difficult as you might think. When you can stand to the side of time and gaze at the hologram as an unbiased observer rather than an active participant, it quickly becomes obvious that anything you can think of can and does exist, but it only has relevance if you force the thought to go through the motions of actually occurring (which also requires a dive into the river Styx, where time has its source).

> **Eliminate time**
> **and you will eliminate death.**

You will be immortal within the energetic body of your Other, because that is your natural state once you shed the programming that tells you otherwise and – also and of great importance – the Other actually *is* the hologram in the sense that it contains all memory/awareness of all experiences... not just your own, but the entirety of the all. You don't remember it all at once (there we go with "time" again) because that isn't how the organism is designed. There might be a better explanation, but in my experiences and observations thus far, I have found no other plausible reason.

To remember "all" at once would be to create the next big bang or big collapse, because the singularity itself is the only "physical" place where time has no real meaning, and there is considerable debate as to whether the inside of a black hole is physical at all, which might explain why time has no place to plant itself in that milieu.

You're asking interesting questions but you might not be asking the *right* question in the right language. Words exist in time. In many ways, words are the language and cornerstones of time. What does the silence of eternity have to say in response to your question?

Our seasons are measured
by the tails and tales of comets,
the breadth and breath
of Lost Tomorrows.

Are We Doomed To Existence?

Even if a seeker doesn't succeed in reaching the immortal condition, their component parts would still remain in existence as recycled energy, right?

The energetic components would remain, but no awareness, no identity, No-thing. Those components that do remain would also be re-distributed so widely that it's unlikely two atoms from the same organism would ever find their way back to one another again, though there is something to be said for quantum entanglement. And at the same time, quantum entanglement clearly does not indicate quantum consciousness. In very clear and indisputable terms: *dead is dead.*

Yes, transcendence would seem to contradict that, but keep in mind that those who transcend aren't recycled except at the purely organic level. Their awareness transfers to the inorganic Other, In that case, dead *isn't* dead.

[[Goddammit, Mikal is contradicting himself again! Fucker!]]

Yes, he is. No he isn't. Think about it.

Is achieving permanent non-existence possible, or is the universe doomed (or gifted, depending on one's perspective) to perpetual, unending existence?

It appears that the universe repeats itself – not necessarily a new and improved universe, but the *same* one cycling through the *same* cycles over and over. *If* that is true, then there is really no such thing as a permanent state of non-existence. That does *not* mean you are already immortal. It only means you *might* be caught in a recurring loop like one of those GIF images that keeps repeating, but with no pause or off button. If you walked down Elm Street at precisely 4:07 pm yesterday, you will do precisely the same thing at precisely the same time and place when the universe recreates herself in a billion times a billion years from now.

It's a rather vast theory (not mine, just one that is commonly discussed). Do I believe it? Sometimes. Seldom. Jury's still out. Now here's the dark part *(What? It wasn't dark enough already?)*

The only real reason the universe would seemingly reset with all components being precisely the same from one manifestation to the next would be if it *is* a program of some sort. A matrix. A computer simulation. A finite loop running on some kid's Speak and Spell in some far distant galaxy (or right next door). Who's to say?

In response to the possibility that our entire reality might be nothing more than pixels on the fabric of cyberspace, some seekers wrote me privately to say it was such a depressing possibility that they found themselves contemplating extensive psychotherapy. But for those who like to twist reality into a knot, it is well worth at least considering, since it forces the mind to think outside the program – *if* that mind has any desire to survive the matrix.

For the record, this isn't *just* some philosophical pondering worthy of drunken nerds at the local pub. It has become a major topic of discussion among respected quantum physicists, many of whom have concluded that it almost certainly *is* a simulation. Look it up. There are countless videos on YouTube (by qualified scientists, not just the usual crackpots), and there are also countless articles by some of those same scientists.

Another thing comes to mind. *If* it is all a simulation and self-replicating at that, repeating over and over as Mikal tends to do when he's trying to make a point, then it would *seem* that attaining the immortal condition would make one immortal into all subsequent manifestations of "the simulation." Then again, who's to say? Immortality is achieved by doing the work, not by default. And personally I choose *not* to believe in predestination as it is commonly understood (though there is little to say it isn't the case, and nothing to say it isn't possible).

As I was composing this, I entered into a private conversation with a good friend, who made the comment, "If it's all a computer simulation, what if the immortals are a virus injected into the program to bring the simulation down completely, or alter it so much that the rules of the game would be permanently changed?"

What if...?

Food for thought.

A chilling reply Mikal. I've two questions now. First, can't you get from gnosis the answers to these questions and reveal them to us? Do you already know them but engage in strategic revealing of information and use of words to cause a reaction in us so we are pushed to discover it all ourselves?

All the immortals I know have done extensive gnosis (and beyond even that) into the original question – "are we doomed to existence?" – and what they have gleaned is essentially what I've told you. However, I will add that only your own gnosis on the subject will have any real relevance, since only then can it be worded or visualized in your own terms through the channels of your own Other.

When I am direct (as I always attempt to be) it is with the hope that my words will shake loose some ancient future memory that will either add to your arsenal of tools on this long and winding road; or perhaps it I am enough of a brutal bastard and you are enough of a hungry hunter, my words might propel you out of the comfort zone of your body and into the embrace of the infinite (transmogrification). To be honest while remaining somewhat modest *[[What? Mikal modest? Right...]]* it wouldn't be the first time that has occurred, and if it is at all even remotely possible to be "turned" by another, that is generally how it is done.

And now I've shared one of the darkest of the dark teachings – that it is the mind/spirit that "turns" and propels the body into the tempest of change, and sometimes (though admittedly rarely) that change can be facilitated by an extant teacher, benefactor, or homeless man mumbling to himself on a street corner. I mean that quite literally.

Occasionally a seeker will transmogrify when abruptly and unexpectedly presented with some truth that leads to understanding that leads to enlightenment that leads to a higher "spin" that leads to transmogrification. Some refer to this as a quantum leap – but in this case it would be an actual leap from organic to inorganic, from mortal to immortal.

So why not just do that? Simple answer: most who make that kind of abrupt transition aren't ready for it and can end up wandering the earth (or the red sands of Mars or the halls of alien starships) mad as any mythical hatter, condemned to suffer that madness until such time (if ever) that their mortal mind makes the transition to immortal being.

Sounds easy? It isn't. It's why any competent teacher doesn't just wave an Ollivander's wand or sink his fangs into the neck of a willing apprentice in order to make them immortal. Could it even be done? Sure. All things are possible, remember? But the teacher also knows the incredible risks and dire consequences if the apprentice falls between the crack between the worlds.

But but but... wouldn't the newly transmogrified immortal eventually settle into their immortality over time? Yes. No. Sometimes. But it's hardly a good way to get there because there is *equal* risk that they might *never* make the transition and – here's a dire bit of consequence for you – they might come to you begging to be terminated. And if you as the teacher *caused* their suffering – whether out of a genuine desire to evolve them or out of your own arrogant ego – it would fall to you to either grant their wish or become their caretaker until such time (if ever) that they stabilize.

But in the meantime, they are like a suffering animal for whom no definitive hope exists. Only a distant and desperate "Maybe it will get better." I do not believe you would allow a beloved pet to suffer in such a manner and so the task that would fall to you would potentially destroy *you* in the process. Not in the sense that it would obliterate your immortality, but in the sense that it would damage your spirit to such an extent that the grief would consume you for whatever length of time eternity might be.

Words are nothing. Yet words have infinite power. They can change you but only when they become more than the sum of their parts.

Will I see what you've been doing all along when I transmogrify and get a keen desire to slap you for all the sleepless nights I spent running around paradoxes? I feel like I might.

Paradoxes are often the key to resolving the paradox. They force the mind to work in a non-linear manner.

Tell me, are those who wish to return to the All (God, the Light, become one with everything) misinterpreting reality, as are those who wish to become nothing?

The concept of becoming one with everything is a program created largely through a misperception and misinterpretation of Eastern mysticism. Be that as it may, the *idea* of returning to the all is real but the act itself is false. (Sufficiently non-sugar-coated?)

The closest one might come to that state is what I have attempted to describe as "the land of the sentient

156

dead[20]." In that state, there is awareness, but without any identity to give it a reference point. There is no "one" to perceive. There is only raw perception. No difference can be made between a supernova and a ladybug on a leaf. Acts of murder are perceived as no different than vows of love. At some level, perhaps that is true, but it is awareness that gives rise to identity and vice versa.

It's easy enough to fall into the land of the sentient dead, but extremely difficult to get out. It cannot even be said that there is a sense of peace or well-being because of the sameness of the All. It could be perceived that those who become part of the land of the sentient dead have achieved non-existence. Another paradox for you.

Attempting to reason out *why* someone might have the desire to become no-thing is pointless speculation. There are a thousand reasons on the head of a pin, but the most common is that they make *no* choice and so the choice is made for them. To *do* nothing is to eventually *be* nothing. Nature even made it easy, you see.

You stated that the mind propels the body to transition. Does this imply the body is merely a projection of the mind?

Depends on where you are standing – whether inside the hologram or outside of it altogether. Keep in mind that the mortal self is the source – the projector if you prefer. The organic self projects consciousness and

---

[20] **Land of the Sentient Dead:** A state of mind/being wherein the *I-Am* (identity) is completely lost and there is only rudimentary awareness. All things in this state are equal, no difference between a magnificent sunset or a comet smashing the earth. No emotional response to anything, just observation without reference points. Without the *I-Am* there is no sense of self. It is only by sheer force of Will that one might be able to resurrect he Self from the mire and step back into a state of cohesive awareness.

experiences awareness, and that is the foundation from which the mind is then *projected* from its organic source into an inorganic quantum state. But that's only the beginning.

> **The mind has the ability to exist outside the body, but only if it is sufficiently nourished and conditioned to become autonomous. That autonomous state is the Other – the sovereign projection of awareness from a corporeal state into a quantum state.**

This is clearly a complex subject. The mortal self projects the mind (an infant) and from there the Other is formed (the infant evolved), and from the Other it could be said (knowing in advance that words are only inadequacies) that the combined experiences of *both* (self and other) conjoin to become the singularity of consciousness[21] – the totality that is eternal, immortal, and capable of projecting the energetic equivalent of a physical body should it have a reason to do so. So as you can see, it isn't a clear-cut one-word answer or even a straightforward walk through time and space. Few things on this twisted road are.

With that foundation in place, *"...does this imply that the body is merely a projection of the mind?"* No. Though most new age woo-woo gurus will tell you otherwise, the mortal body *does* come first. The body projects the mind, which creates the Other, who can then project a body. Ouroboros.

---

[21] **Singularity of Consciousness:** The self made Whole, the evolution of consciousness which results in a cohesive field of awareness existing ubiquitously and non-locally, infinitely and eternally, but with the ability to localize if necessary or desired. The immortal condition. The cohesive, fully integrated *I-Am* consisting of all components of the mortal self and the eternal Other, brought together under a single assemblage point. The individuated totality of oneself.

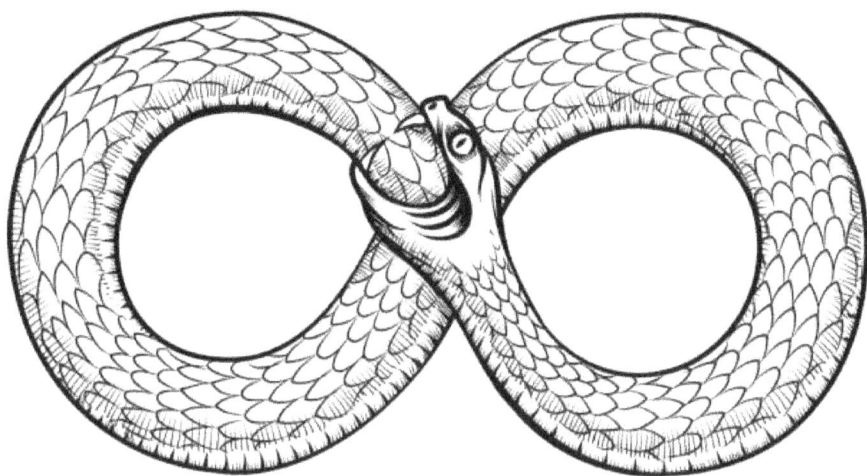

Why do so many woo-woo gurus get it wrong? Because they have no words to describe the creation of the Other from a quantum perspective, and because they are perceiving time in a linear manner even if they might intuitively Know otherwise. End result, it *appears* on the surface of linear thinking that the mind descends into the body at the moment of conception, but the reality of it is altogether different, as anyone who has been on this path for very long knows by now.

There is no line-up of wise old spirits waiting to take a red-eye down to Earth to hop into a fetus. But it's a much *easier* explanation than trying to follow the complex progression from sperm/egg into an eventual immortal being.

The woo-woo guru explanation also suffers from a fatal (literally) flaw. If you are already immortal, inhabited by an immortal spirit who jumped into you before you were born, then 1) there is no need to do *any* amount of work because you are *already* immortal; and 2) if that immortal spirit already existed and merely inhabited your wee-fetus, then who the hell are *you* without the presence of this hitchhiking ghost in the machine? Questions for another dark night, but nonetheless questions that need to be considered in the context of this discussion.

You said before the mind isn't located in the brain, so where is it then? (Please oh please don't say non-local.)

It is non-local.

The mind doesn't exist until awareness amasses experience – even if that experience is one of floating serenely in its mother's womb. It's been debated since the rise of The First Fundamental Lie as to when/where consciousness begins. It is perhaps impossible to pinpoint the moment, and ultimately it makes little difference. The mind functions *through* the brain in the same way songs play over a radio. But you won't find a bunch of moldy oldy bands *inside* the radio anymore than you will find the mind *inside* the brain.

Does that mean the mind is already pure energy?

In a milieu where time is The First Fundamental Lie, there is no "already" in the equation. And for that matter, all things are pure energy at their core. From the perspective of *if* we are a computer simulation, then it stands to reason that all things are pure energy at their core, for then it would also follow that all things are only pixels and static on some rusty old PC running in an abandoned lab, forgotten by time itself.

Does this mean there is a "physical" universe outside of the simulation? Maybe. Maybe not. Certainly no simple way to know. For if *we* are a simulation, there is nothing to indicate that the ones running the simulation aren't a simulation themselves, and so the rabbit's hole spirals deeper and deeper into speculation until the mind folds in on itself and becomes a cricket on the shoulder of a madman.[22]

The mind in its infant stage is the storage container for perception, the processing center for awareness. It might sound like those are functions of the physical brain, but while there might be some rudimentary truth to that, the mind is more accurately the synapses between the physical neurons. The mind is the receptacle of the individual unit's (that would be *you*) combined experiences – both those it can perceive directly and those it can only intuit.

It is from that intuitive aspect that the mind begins to take on its own characteristics, its innate curiosity, and – eventually – its awareness that it is a finite organism that will die if it doesn't figure out a way to exceed its natural matrix and become Other than the accumulation of its organic tidbits.

When the mind recognizes that simple truth is when it begins to project the Other. Or, when it folds its wings, goes back to sleep, and encourages the body to sit on the couch all day, eating Cheetohs and playing soul-numbing games as a way to distract them both (mind/body) from the hardcore realization that spirit (the third element) is not a gift handed out at the moment of conception. It is instead something that must be generated through curiosity and love-of-life, perfected through actual Work, and inhabited through a lifetime of Intent culminating in a transformative blaze of pure Will (transmogrification or transcension).

---

[22] **Ancestor simulation:** For a more scientific (and actually humorous) look at the idea of all of this being a computer simulation, this is just one video I found to be entertaining.. Nice to know Neil deGrasse Tyson has a fine sense of humor. https://www.youtube.com/watch?v=hmVOV7xvl58 For those reading the paperback, go to YouTube and type in the description: "Are We Living In An Ancestor Simulation."

Putting 'Reality' on the Exam Table

From a quantum and timeless perspective, anything you can imagine already exists as a thoughtform, even those things typically considered unreal. This doesn't mean you are likely to encounter a unicorn in your bathtub or a dragon egg in your box of cereal. It merely means that all things are equally real and equally unreal, depending largely on where you are standing inside the jaws of linear time.

From a letter to an apprentice...

If we're going to discuss reality, it's important we agree what reality is and therein lies its fallacy. A wooden table is solid enough, but in a thousand years it will crumble to dust, as unreal as it was before the seed was planted from which the tree grew so the table could be spun whole by mortal hands that could thump on the wood and proclaim it "real," when in reality it was a transient thing; and if the mortal survived those thousand years until the table disappeared, would he argue it was real because it had been there once (even though it was there no more) and if his past perceptions tripped over the phantom leg of where that table once stood would he stub his toe enough to make it bleed?

What was the nature of the table's reality? It came from nothing and to nothing returned, for before it was a seed dropped from a tree, it was nothing if not nothing at all, and what is that but magic creating itself and calling it "nature" to satisfy the consensual continuum with a word more politically correct? Scientifically we can explain it all from stamen and pollen to seed to tree to table to dust, but the real conundrum is this: before the table existed it did not exist, but was part of a future reality; and after the table crumbles to nothing it no longer exists, so how are human perceptions to confirm it ever existed at all or argue it was any more real when it occupied molecular space? (And why oh why does the reality of "reality" concern the mortals so much?)

Ah, but even if it doesn't exist does that make it unreal, for now there's the legend of the table sung into being by those who remember it, and what created the thing if not mortals who needed a table upon which to place their faith in reality?

– March, 1996

Reality is an old man in lace panties, nibbling on a giant lollipop bought for a penny from a drunken harlequin at the Circus of the Happily Damned. (And now even that is real... You're welcome.)

Is the Program Sentient?

The universe is altogether impersonal and doesn't give half a distant damn about you or me or the man on the Martian moon. What *is* real is the consensus and the programs that arise out of it. It could be argued either way as to whether the programs become sentient over time.

*What **is** The Program? I hear a lot of people talking about it but can anyone really define it?*

- Women over 30 shouldn't have long hair.
- There is a right way and a wrong way to Be.
- Certain words should not be used even though they were okay yesterday. Get with the program!

- God is on *our* side. (I read it on Facebook, so obviously it's true!)
- The needs of the many outweigh the needs of the One (unless I am the one asked to wear a mask or vaccinate my crotch goblins.)
- All things die.
- There's no such thing as ghosts, vampires or things that go bump in the night.
- Get with the program.
- If you're not for me, you're against me.
- If I don't get it right this time around, there's always my next life.
- Get with the program.

All you have to do is examine your reactions to life, the universe and everything in between as it all unfolds before you like a beautiful flower with an often poisonous scent.

> **The Program is what you believe without even knowing you believe it. It is the intrinsic core of your foundation, the puppet strings of your mortal identity until such time as you gnaw through the tethers, turn your back on your puppet masters, and walk free into the world as an unfettered being.**

Is that even possible?

Yes. No. Sometimes. The real challenge is undoing not only the hidden programs, but following their roots to the deeper levels that came into this world with you, perhaps as a byproduct of racial memory itself, or perhaps just some set of morals and standards inadvertently shoved up your chute at a very early age by parents, grandparents, clammy-handed preachers, and rosary-fumbling prayer-mumbling nannies.

164

It's not really your fault, but it's a death sentence if you don't *see* it sooner rather than later, and go through the hard work of shaking it off the way a wet dog shakes off the rancid water after falling into a cesspool.

And of course, The Program is designed (not by intelligent design but by lazy default) to convince you that "shaking it off" would mean you are a right ripe lunatic who must now atone for his sins in the darkest corner of some padded room in some green-walled institution for the criminally insane.

You have defied The Program.

You have been a very naughty boy and now you must be spanked soundly and turned into an example lest others follow in your deeply misguided footsteps.

You are a lawbreaker and a boat-rocker and if you will not relent and toe the line, no good will come of it. Or you. This path you're on is a dead end and it will cost you everything, young man. Including your very life.

And so you are marched ceremoniously to the guillotine – whether real or only figurative – and your balls are chopped off, followed quickly by your head. If you live, it is as a zombie walking the earth, mouthing all the right words and phrases pre-determined by The Program, while everything you once were lies cold and dead at the altar of Proper Society.

The Program does not tolerate dissent because, despite its flag-waving demonstrations of right and might, it is actually very fragile because it is dependent on a gestalt that is constantly changing, even if not necessarily evolving or growing. The morals and standards of today are not the same as those of a century ago, regardless of the fact that they are both spawned in the same stagnant sea of consensually-held beliefs. And what is held sacred today will be dust in the wind of tomorrow in the same way that what your grandparents or even your parents considered gospel is now largely regarded as prejudice, bigotry, racism and misogyny, just to name a few.

The Program has learned to adapt, but it never *changes* much. It is the flagship of the absurd belief that "The majority rules." But by virtue of that very thing, it is also the *sinking* ship that must be continually bailing water out of *Titanic* with a child's plastic bucket and a teacup. It is, in essence, the collective unconscious belief systems of the lowest common denominator of the human population.

With that settled, there is The Program and then there are the lesser programs that operate like sub-domains within the larger milieu.

Some immortals say the programs are just recordings, like bad rap music. I have seen evidence which indicates that some programs take on an independence that isn't exactly intelligence, but is a instinctual survival mechanism which causes the program to fight for its sovereign existence.

Religion is one, particularly Catholicism just to use one example. Possession and exorcism are battles between the program (Catholicism) and the rebellion (so-called Satan) and it can never be predicted which side will win in any random battle. Examples in society are prevalent and require only a brief glance to recognize. Politics. Morals (which trend with the times and are one driving force that compels The Program to adapt.). Sex (there's a right way and a wrong way, and a long list of who you can screw and who you can't, usually involving gender or genitalia). And on and deeper into the spiral the closer you look.

I would therefore say the larger Program becomes a tulpa of sorts. The difference is that when the tulpa is fueled by millions or billions of people's energy, that tulpa can and does become a quantifiable force capable of creating quantifiable results. Such is the nature of "Agent Smith" – a self-created and seemingly self-aware

166

aspect of the program spun into existence as an attempt by The Program to protect itself.

When this begins to occur, it is a sure sign that The Program has become top-heavy and – as the humans might say – "too big for its britches." It is therefore destined to fall, but the dark side is that when it does, it tends to take entire civilizations with it because humans become disoriented and disconnected when their collective beliefs are threatened.

This is precisely why world governments have traditionally resisted the idea of releasing irrefutable evidence of the existence of extraterrestrials. Such information could result not so much in panic, but in a total collapse of the prevailing beliefs of a huge segment of the population. How so? For example, if it were to be discovered that the aliens were actually the ones who originally seeded Earth, any notion of God could theoretically be swept right out the airlock.

When it was initially proven that the Earth isn't flat, many people couldn't wrap their head around such an idea and essentially lost their minds. As long as the flat Earth was at the center of the universe and God was smiling down on the human race from heaven, all was right with the world. But when that paradigm shifted and it was further proven that the Earth was nowhere near the center of the universe and heaven could not be located even with the most powerful telescopes, many began to lose their faith and – in my own humble opinion – this was the beginning of the end of the collective human soul.

It matters not in the least that God is a fictional character and heaven a fanciful location like Narnia or Hogwarts. *[[Hogwarts isn't fictional, Mikal. Stop saying that shit!]]*

What matters is that humans as a whole *need* to believe in something greater than themselves – something that watches over them and takes their side in battles and opens its doors to their soul when this mortal life is over. And when those beliefs are stripped from them with evidence that cannot be refuted, the inevitable result is fear, depression, anger, and relentless hatred of whoever broke the spokes of their pretty red tricycle.

So what's the solution?

Either unplug the machine before it explodes or be elsewhere when the explosion occurs. Study the fine art of talking The Program to death as Captain Kirk often did in old episodes of *Star Trek.*

Photo copyright © Paramount Pictures

When The Program reaches a point where it can no longer control its subjects, it self-destructs, but the fallout is often catastrophic to all life, or at least to the existing *way* of life.

The only other option is to be immune to the fallout – to become *that-which-cannot-die.* Of course, the responsibility that comes with such a state is incomprehensible. And again the spiral spirals deeper and colder into the dark.

When you say "unplug the machine before it explodes" is this even possible? Or, rather, isn't it more likely that a person would have a better chance of unplugging themselves from the machine?

Yes, that would be another way of looking at it. As a bit of back story, one of my apprentices believes all lifeforms (at least those on Earth) are individual cells of the machine, and that the machine itself is an organism moving through space and time. The Program is created by the hive mind of the organic machine (similar to Jung's idea of the collective unconscious).

We have discussed that it is possible for individual cells to either break away from the gestalt, or in extreme circumstances, unplug or short-circuit the entire machine itself. If you were able to trace things back through time, it would be observed that Rome fell because *one* person at some point planted a seed that created such a conflict within the machine that the machine and its directive were unable to repair themselves, and so the machine became unplugged from... *itself*.

There have been several such instances throughout history wherein the organic machine becomes too top-heavy and therefore susceptible to destruction from within the framework of its own matrix. Some have argued that the machine is aware of its flaws and destroys itself through this inner self-destruct mechanism, while others stand firm on the belief that one individual cell has the power to disrupt and destroy the entire machine, given sufficient motive (even if the cell is not aware of its power at the time).

> **Cancer begins with a single cell and so does insurrection.**

In the bigger picture, it might not matter, but if the theory that one cell can unplug the entire machine is accurate, it is potentially strong validation for the realization that you really *are* the most powerful being in the universe.

I personally perceive The Program to be ubiquitous, at least insofar as it would pertain to life on Earth. The "programs" are transient belief systems that take on a life of their own, but a life that is usually every bit as transient and mortal as those who spawn it. Put another way, what humanity believes today is almost always considered foolish tomorrow.

I find it at once devastatingly savage, cruel, and also interesting that The Program seems to be able to continually resurrect and repair itself and grow out of control time and time again.

It appears to be a pattern of long-standing, stretching as far back as recorded time. When one program becomes too top-heavy, it collapses, taking with it all who were plugged into it.

The *big* Program is no different. There will come a time (there always does) when human consciousness makes a dramatic shift and the existing paradigm is no longer viable. Often that shift is caused by one individual – someone with sufficient awareness to manifest a ripple in the force, which grows as it spreads outward from the source. When the ripple becomes greater than The Program, The Program capsizes and those most deeply affected scramble to reassemble their world, creating in the process a "new and improved" paradigm that is really only a walking dead resurrection of the old one, even if wrapped in a shiny tin foil hat.

The only way it seems to *totally* self destruct is when the universe (as it is commonly perceived) collapses in on itself and begins the process all over again. It does indeed seem the world is teetering on the edge of a personal collapse, probably a return to a much more primitive time if things continue as they are going.

I'm still mulling over the idea of the individual cell breaking away from The Program being what destroys it. Definitely for that individual, The Program is destroyed, yet as a whole, unless "infected" with some kind of discord or some event that sets in motion the domino effect of certain destruction (as in your Rome example) The Program wouldn't be destroyed. Would it?

It is actually that domino effect which collapses The Program. It's why prophets and naysayers were put to death in the past (and even in the now). Those who wake up the others are not looked upon with kindness, for they have the power to cause that ripple effect which has the potential to bring the whole thing grinding to a halt.

If the Will of one is so powerful, that's not enough? I wonder if The Program can be unplugged before doomsday.

It is very true that One can cause a ripple – even a major one. I've seen it. In small ways, I've even done it. But if the ripple is confined only to a fish bowl, it will make no difference in the end. The butterfly flapping his wings in Brazil really *doesn't* cause the hurricane in Bali. It's a nice visual representation of how energy works, and yet... energy doesn't *really* work that way. It would take more than one butterfly, you see, and over a longer period of time than any single butterfly will fly on this magnificent Earth.

The Program will never be unplugged – not entirely. Sorry to squash any fragile hopes hanging out there, but The Program is intrinsic to the human race. It is part of who "they" are as a unit, part of how they function.

Seekers have a minute chance to *escape* the program, but again it is normally just The One, who might or might not choose to teach others to follow or drag them kicking and screaming out of their box (which generally only works for a short time).

To better understand the very nature of reality, think on these things in whatever you do that passes for meditation.

How did Neo unplug the program?

What is it in the matrix that holds *you* prisoner?

What tools do you possess to unplug yourself?

———

This is the secret to evolution – the turning of the frequency from finite to infinite, death to life. There is no margin for error here. This is the truth which underlies all immortality: the willful choice to become a penthouse resident of the universe instead of only renting a transient room on the ground floor for a brief interlude which humans call a life.

PART FIVE
Seducing the Other

*Together we shall grow old
and outlive Death and Time.*

———

The Other
The Link Between Here and the Eternal Now

*You've talked a lot about the Other, referring to it as
the double or the energy body or the dreaming body or
the twin. What I'd like to know is this: Is it a quantifiable
entity or more like a hypothetical one such as the idea of
the human soul?*

It is both. It is neither. And it would depend entirely
on your definitions of quantifiable vs. hypothetical or
allegorical. It has been recognized by the immortals that
we live in a world of duality[23] wherein two seemingly
contradictory states may exist side by side without
either threatening the sovereignty of the other.

But to give you as much of a straightforward answer
as possible, the Other begins as a spark in the same
way a massive fire begins with the strike of a single
match. As the seeker grows and evolves, the spark
grows and evolves as well – becoming a projection of

---

[23] **Duality**: Meaning, literally, "two things simultaneously". Duality implies the
evolving perception which enables us to see that past and future are no different,
but only different perceptions according to our location in time. Duality further
allows for two seemingly contradictory conditions to exist simultaneously, without
either obliterating or usurping the other. Duality can be studied in the statement,
"You must *be* immortal before you will know how to *become* immortal."

energy emanating originally from the mortal source, but gradually through unconditional love and nurturing, becoming a powerful force in its own right. I use the word 'force' because there really is nothing in the English language that adequately describes the true nature of the Other. The essence, purpose, and agenda of the Other has been discussed at greater length in _Darker Teachings of the Immortals_, but briefly, the Other is the energetic vessel of your awareness beyond mortal life – a vessel which is reached either through transmogrification or transcendence.

It is also a great deal more than that, serving as teacher, mentor, guide, and occasionally even as tormentor and personal devil when necessary to keep the seeker on track. This mentorship generally occurs through the process known as silent knowing, or gnosis, though there have been many cases of seekers encountering their Other in the flesh – whether they knew it at the time or not.

> *Time has given me*
> *ten thousand faces,*
> *and I have donned*
> *ten thousand masks*
> *to hide the madness*
> *in these immortal eyes.*

Downloading the Other

I've read a lot about downloading the Other into the human form so one might have access to the Other's vast knowledge and abilities. On the other hand, is that wise?

This is a questionable and perhaps even dangerous idea making the rounds, largely through the efforts of others who have begun writing about potential

174

immortality, but who clearly have no personal experience.

The Other is a construct of energy – immortal, eternal, ubiquitous. The mortal self is an organic construct – mortal, finite, confined to its meat suit for the most part. It should be obvious that the seeker would strive to transfer mortal awareness into the immortal structure – and *not* the other way around.

> **The Other is the vessel of your immortality. Bringing it into a mortal structure would be akin to moving the entire contents of the Louvre into a crumbling ruin with no roof and no security system.**

Can it be done? Of course it *can* be done, but except for situations of dire and immediate emergency, it would be a foolhardy proposition at best. The logic used by proponents of "downloading the Other" is that it gives the seeker greater access to the double's power and abilities – particularly with regard to so-called "magical powers." And why is it that so many who seek after immortality think it involves becoming the superhero of the week?

First of all, that supposition isn't even remotely true for several reasons, not the least of which is that the human brain/mind doesn't possess the capacity to contain the kind of knowledge the Other possesses. It would be like trying to download the latest version of Windows onto an old Commodore 64. And if you're wondering what the 64 means, it means 64K of RAM. Hardly sufficient to handle the proposed task.

Are there situations where you might *need* to bring your Other into your mortal self? Perhaps, but when those circumstances arise, it is generally observed that the Other does what it needs to do without a conscious directive on the part of the mortal self. And under those circumstances, the Other can come and go as necessary, as opposed to being possibly trapped within a decaying mortal form.

Can the double be trapped in a mortal body? Anything is possible. While the double is essentially self-willed, it also is tethered to the organic mortal self and if that organic mortal self is sufficiently stubborn, there is a possibility that the Other could be more or less imprisoned – *not because it* <u>couldn't</u> *escape, but because the mortal self decides its own fate.*

For those who like to read every book ever written on the subject of immortality – buyer beware. I would even include my own books in that caveat. What is true is usually only true if one *makes* it true – if one forces something to go through the motions of actually occurring.

The Driving Force

When I started the path I couldn't understand how the love for my Other could be the driving force. After so many times she's appeared in my dreams I'm finally starting to get it but I still can't think of her as an actual being/person/immortal.

The greatest mystery and the greatest conundrum you will ever consider is that of the Other. There is no predicting when or even if the seeker will encounter their Other within the timeframe of their mortal life, or if the Other will remain elusive and behind the veil – ever-present and undeniable, but at the same time nebulous and *seemingly* unreachable.

From what I have observed, it depends largely on the seeker's predilections. Those who are more naturally open to the mystical and the unexplainable are perhaps *less* likely to encounter their Other in the flesh because they do not need convincing that such things are real and possible. Instead, those seekers strive primarily to work with their Other through dreaming, meditation and gnosis.

In any sort of dealings with the Other, energy is a key factor, and it takes a considerable amount of energy for the Other to manifest in seemingly "physical" form because the *source* of the Other's energy is at least partially connected to the mortal self until such time as transmogrification or transcension occurs. That is a *very* limited explanation.

While some doubles *can* manifest with ease or even run the length of time and space with no negative consequences, most simply can't, particularly in the early stages of the seeker's journey. Therefore, expending large amounts of energy unless absolutely necessary is not common, and definitely not recommended.

The type of seeker who is perhaps more firmly grounded in practicality and a more logical/scientific view of the world is seemingly *more* likely to be hit over the head with at least one encounter with their Other – though I should make it very clear that such encounters usually don't take any sort of straightforward manifestation. In some cases, the Other might inhabit a seemingly solid human form, taking the manifestation of a stranger one might meet in some mundane setting. Other times, the Other might inhabit the form of an existing human (skinwalking[24]), assuming an appropriate form can be found, and the human host would agree to the exchange of energy. The primary reason the Other would choose to manifest in such a blatant form usually has to do with breaking through

---

[24] **Skinwalker:** A being who has the ability to temporarily inhabit the body of another. In certain branches of shamanism, the shaman may invite an evolved entity (often his own double) to inhabit his body for the purpose of sharing consciousness and expanding awareness. While certain religious groups have expressed a fear of this as a form of possession, skinwalking is normally a mutual agreement between the seeker and the entity or spirit to whom he would lend his body. Do unscrupulous skinwalkers exist? Sure. So do unscrupulous priests.

the stubborn programs that many seekers possess, even if they don't want to, even if they might believe they are open to the unknown.

With that said, the Other *can* manifest at any time for any reason, but there are certain dangers inherent to this. As don Juan cautioned Carlos Castaneda, "The sorcerer who comes face to face with his double is a dead sorcerer." And while that might not be entirely true in every situation, it is true enough. Why? Because the instinct to conjoin totally is so all-consuming that it is like the gravity of a black star – and if the seeker isn't ready to make the leap, there is a strong possibility they won't survive a face-to-face meeting with the Other.

The possibilities are endless, and so there is a natural tendency for the Other to remain always out of reach, but with the promise that – one fine night – that distance will be breached and when the two *do* come together, it will be the birth of a new star in the form of the singularity of consciousness.

Come.
Night will be our playground,
the stars our unborn children.

There is a story about Goethe meeting his own double out on the road one night. Other authors have written about similar experiences. The real key to surviving such an experience seems to rest in the fact that most who do meet their double in the flesh have no idea at the time that it *is* their double, thereby activating the old cliché "Ignorance is bliss." Or "What you don't know won't hurt you." Not always truth, but true enough in this situation.

So again I would say it depends largely on the seeker's predilections and practices. If the mindset of a seeker is *too* firmly anchored in "the real world" the Other will take whatever steps are necessary to shake it loose so that it might experience the ineffable and, in

178

doing so, come to terms with the idea of allowing what was rigidly believed to be impossible.

The Other is a ruthless trickster and will stop at nothing, for the simple reason that they are fighting for their life as much as the seeker is fighting for theirs. When you give the Other free rein to teach you and make you immortal, there are no longer any restrictions on what the Other might do.

Remember, Remember
The art of making it real

Mikal recently said that remembering is the act of creation – when we actually remember something as opposed to only daydreaming it, it's coming from a different part of the brain and so it will have very real effects.

I once had an apprentice who managed to transmogrify within a span of just over 5 years. I was recently asked how he managed this, since it often seems to take much longer. Was it a matter of isolating himself or doing something different than most seekers might think to do?

Mark (I'll call him that for now) didn't completely isolate himself from the real world, as he held a job for purely survival reasons, though that was more or less his total social interaction. When not at work, he was either reading or spending his time in contemplation – I wouldn't call it actual meditation, since it wasn't about clearing the mind as much as about pondering a specific question or aspect of the journey.

In our conversations over the years, I had given him the task of "Remember what I will do to you." Words I have shared with several apprentices, but which may be interpreted in many different ways. And ultimately it's not about *anything* I would do or even *could* do. The only one who can turn you is *you*. But if you choose to believe in immortality rituals and benevolent immortal Creators, that can also be a powerful tool.

> **To actively remember something is to place it in the area of the brain/mind associated with reality. You remember what you had for breakfast, so it is real to you. You remember what you dreamed last night, but the brain/mind classifies it as "not-real," so even though you concede that the *dream* was real, you conclude that the *content* was not.**

The act of truly remembering is the act of *creating* the memory – generating the visuals, feelings, consequences and outcome of the event – and then giving it life by placing it in the area of the brain/mind associated with so-called "real memories" as opposed to "dream memories" (just for example).

Mark focused on those words until eventually they began to take on a life of their own. It wasn't just imagining what I might do to him that would mysteriously change him from a mortal state to a quantum state, it was a matter of *remembering* what had been *done* – placing the event in the "past" so that it would be *seen* as *already* accomplished.

He said he needed to remember it as a physical act brought about by an extant creator. My response? Whatever it takes. So in his meditations and contemplations, he would focus on trying to generate that memory. At first, he said he could only capture tiny glimpses of it. In this context, I was someone he had known for awhile, a friend with whom he occasionally shared drinks at a local Irish pub. (He was keen on detail). Over time, the details slowly expanded when he was able to concentrate on one aspect and take it from there to the next step.

It took him about 4 years of intense focus to retrieve (manifest) the whole memory, and when he did, he stood face to face with his choice. Did he put it aside as an exercise in visualization (consigning it to the role of fantasy) or did he accept it as an *actual* memory, committing himself to transmogrification because according to his memory, the event had *already* happened and by that logic, he was already transformed. He chose the latter despite his very natural human fears, and made the leap one starry night in the middle of spring.

The hard part is getting past the language that is embedded in one's operating system. Humans think of remembering as a passive dalliance, which is one definition. But if the word "remember" is transformed to a command, an active and relentless *force*, it takes on the elements of creating a Creator.

Something I recently said to an apprentice: "You have to *be* immortal before you can know how to *become* immortal – for it is only from the immortal perspective that you can remember what is going to happen that will change you forever. Once you Remember, the deed is done. But because it is the Other who moves outside of time, it is from his perspective that actual memory of his past and your future create the bridge between mortal and immortal. Remember from *his* perspective and you will know not only how to *become* immortal, but how you *became* immortal."

When you can open your eyes inside the Other, head straight for that memory if you dare. That is where you will find yourSelf.

A tale of power if you choose to believe it, or just a fairy tale if not.

———

181

Light your twisted candles.
Call me by my name.
Invite me in,
knowing I've been here
all along.

A Musing

What you need to understand about the Other is that it is as elusive as a sprite – mischievous fiend that runs when you chase it, hides when you think you've found it, disappears just when you are about to catch it. Not to worry. It has nothing to do with you. This is simply its nature – what it *must* do if you are to do the Do-ing that will bring the unruly creature to your side when you need it most. Not because you are lonely or sad or aching to be loved, but when you need a sanctuary to run to when Death comes knocking at your door.

It isn't the Other's automatic nature to love you or need you. Quite the other way around, and this is not because nature is cruel or god is a tyrant (though both are generally true) but because it is the love you have for the Other that makes them whole and gives them the agenda to make *you* whole in return.

> **You create the Other**
> **so that the Other may then create you.**

You nurture the Other with ache/hurt/want/need (all forms of intense energy), and when the hurt feels unbearable is when the Other rises up out of the darkness to take his first immortal breath, so that he may, in turn, breathe that life into you when the brute with the scythe is hot on your tail and your earthly tale is done.

It's a courtship that might drive you mad. It's a love affair that, once consummated through the immortal Other's embrace, will last an eternity and beyond.

What *is* the immortal's embrace? Simply this... it is the first shared breath that changes you forever, when the mortal self takes his last breath (transmogrification or transcension being the same in this case) and the immortal Other inhales the totality of it all into himself... creator and created, dancer and the dance, each consuming the other and rising as the phoenix from the ashes.

Will it hurt?

If it didn't I dare say it would not be real, for this depth of love is as much agony as ecstasy.

The lines in my palm
foretell starfalls and comet trails
while mortals come and go,
fleeting snow flurries.

The Other and Earthly Relationships

Can you say a bit about relationships between seekers, and how it can strengthen the relationship to the twin?

Relationships on any level are tricky sticky wickets more likely to burn the house to the ground than provide a steady warm glow. Such is the nature of human nature. I have known couples (both of whom were seekers) who formed a relationship bond rooted primarily in the intent to channel and experience their Others. Some of these relationships were platonic. Others (most) became highly intimate, sexual, even tantric. Any or all of those manifestations are fine unto themselves, but they can come with a long list of potential complications – more or less affecting the mortal selves.

It goes something like this Let's say Alice and Alex are both seekers and find themselves moderately attracted to one another. They decide to proceed with a cautious relationship, but pretty soon each of them realizes their Other is beginning to use the relationship as a means to "speak up." This might be called channeling or "tapping in" or whatever label feels best without sounding utterly insane.

The couple find themselves speaking/acting/projecting from the assemblage point *of* the Other, and often this progresses into a very real need for consummation – if not sexual, at least physical on some level. The relationship between the mortal couple deepens, but primarily through the two Others. Maybe Alice doesn't even really *like* Alex because he wears a bow tie and is known to recite bad poetry at the pub. Maybe Alex doesn't particularly like Alice because she has her hair in a mullet and listens to sappy old hippie music in her beat-up Ford Pinto. But their Others might be "in love" – or, more precisely, their Others are being spiritually nurtured by the process of being given full rein to "step forward".

The problems here should be obvious. The relationship between the mortal couple probably isn't sustainable in the long-term, *but* it is of incredible value to *all* parties (mortal selves and immortal Others) for the time the wild hayride of emotional overload lasts. With seekers, it is sometimes possible to enter into such a relationship with the knowledge that it is to serve a purpose rather than being intended as a lifelong commitment. In the same way tantric sex may occur between strangers who are physically compatible, so it is with relationships among seekers that may develop for the purpose of "channeling the Other."

*Do the feelings between the two earthly parties
always help to strengthen the feelings and connection
with the twin of each party?*

Sometimes, maybe, who's to say? It depends largely
on the two parties and what their individual goals might
be. I've known couples who found the foundation in the
mortal world to form a permanent, committed
relationship. I've known others who lasted a few
months, maybe even a year or two, but eventually went
their separate ways.

The act of "channeling the Other" could also be
likened to sexual role playing (though it's far above that
despite surface appearances). When you surrender
yourself to your Other completely, you might become
the Other as they were in the year 1525, when
captaining a pirate ship on the high seas. You might
become your Other as they will be in the year 2510
(keeping in mind that "time" is irrelevant), when they
will be standing on the black sands of Rigel 7 just for
the joy of watching the fireflies come up out of the
ground in the night.

It is impossible to predict how such manifestations
of the Other will happen through the outward
expression of gnosis. But one thing is certain: it is just
one more way in which the Other shows you who *you*
are and what you are becoming.

As for your partner in such adventures... one will
have a tendency to lead, the other a tendency to follow.
So if Alice's Other heads off to Rigel 7, chances are
Alex's Other will follow and share in the experience. The
Other is omnipresent, so it can move from one location
to another at Will.

*Does the twin ever manipulate situations so that it
brings a person into the seeker's life, knowing they will
be beneficial for the seeker's path and twin connection?*

Absolutely. Not every stranger you meet on the street is a stranger.

What about physical intimacy, does intimacy between the two earthy parties also strengthen the connection to the Other? Can it be detrimental in some cases?

Physical intimacy is definitely a possibility, but not always a necessity. It depends on the Intent of the mortal parties *and* on the Intent of the two Others involved. The Other can have agendas that it doesn't share with its mortal self because if it *did*, the mortal self would run screaming and hide under the bed for the rest of its life.

The important thing for seekers to remember is that nothing is ever as it seems. Sometimes you have to take a risk to get a reward – and sometimes that risk will break your heart even though the reward might be considered worthwhile in the end.

The other important thing is to take the energy that comes from such a situation and use it in accordance with your higher intent. What*ever* happens, it's not wasted if it enables the Other to peek out from the shadows for a moment and give you a glimpse of who you really are behind all those mortal masks and machinations.

Are such relationships dangerous? Of course. Anything worth doing comes with risks. What matters is that you emerge from the experience without bitterness or regret, but with new Knowledge.

———

Ravens will be my eyes upon you,
mist my dangerous caress.

Meddling With the Other of Others

As an immortal who exists beyond time, are you able to meet, see, know, interact with seekers' Others "before" the seeker in the now becomes immortal? If so, do you act as a guide to the Other as well, working as mentor to the whole being rather than just the mortal source? Or do you stay away for the most part, letting each individual Other learn/grow/explore and figure it out for itself? (Have I opened a can of worms?)

There have been occasions wherein I have connected with an apprentice's Other before the apprentice achieved the immortal condition, though it is rare and requires me to have an intimate working knowledge of the apprentice's status, progress and, for lack of a better word, prognosis. It is occasionally possible under those circumstances for an immortal to provide instruction and impetus to the Other, particularly when the Other is not yet entirely Whole and could be "indecisive" – always the result of a reflection of its mortal self.

As one dark but brief example, if the Other shows too much leniency toward the mortal self, chances are high that the mortal will never make the transition to immortality. In that case, an existing immortal is often able to provide guidance and at times may even imbue the fledgling Other with Knowledge and an injection of power in the form of intense animus, which enables the Other to be as ruthless in its dealings with the mortal source as it is loving.

And somewhere in that dark equation arises the statement, "You created me to create you." It is only when the mortal self surrenders to the Other that transmogrification can occur – and usually that surrender can only happen when the Other has gained sufficient power to force the transition to go through the motions of actually occurring.

The can of worms this might open is that the Other is like any other work in progress – it has a beginning, a middle, and a moment of completion wherein it then exists as the completely viable energetic structure, both within the apprentice and simultaneously within the super position of the assemblage point – omnipresent throughout the space-time continuum and beyond.

Once the Other attains that status, it can navigate the immortal realm even before the mortal self transmogrifies – which is how it gains sufficient Knowledge and awareness to be the mentor and the Creator the mortal self requires in order to make the leap from organic to inorganic.

So this would be for someone you're close to and in frequent contact with? Scarier question: How do you determine someone's prognosis? Would you only do that if you had some personal, vested interest in making sure that person succeeds?

Generally it has involved someone close to me, usually an advanced apprentice. To determine someone's prognosis is fairly easy and is a matter of observing them and how they react to life situations, questions I might pose to them, and a host of other stimuli. It doesn't have to be a personal interest to me – and other than on extremely rare occasion, I have no vested interest in making sure anyone succeeds. I lean toward potential I see in some but not necessarily in others.

Those who are always looking for shortcuts or primarily interested in super powers might be highly motivated individuals here in the Now, but might otherwise have low potential for survival in the immortal world because it is probably not going to be in alignment with what they were hoping. There is simply no point in helping someone achieve the immortal

188

condition if they are only going to bring their earthbound limitations with them.

This is perhaps a good opportunity to look at the role of Will in the dark equation. When your Will finally moves – and there is no way to predict when or even if this will ever occur – is when transmogrification will happen in an instant. The Other doesn't always hesitate because s/he isn't ready or even because they might sense that you aren't ready. They hesitate because the Will has not been activated. I truly wish there was an easy way to command the Will into action, but there is none that I have encountered.

A lot of new age woo-woo goo-roos talk about "summoning the will" but that is a fallacy. Will is an active, moving, mysterious force. It comes when you least expect it, and often when you most need it, but at the same time it is elusive and unpredictable. Anyone who tells you otherwise is trying to sell you an expensive workshop in some exotic location.

It is also questionable as to which aspect of the self will experience the movement of Will – whether the will of the Other or the will of the mortal self. It can go either way.

Is there no way for the apprentice to know if this moment of completion and surrender has occurred?

There is no definitive way that could be quantified, but the apprentices I have worked with have what amounts to a moment of internal surrender wherein things become completely clear and the Way forward is seen. At that juncture, the literal point of no return has been reached and transmogrification proceeds with or without one's conscious permission – which was given way back in the dim times when one first gave their Other free rein to do what must be done, "no matter what." As the old saying goes, be careful what you witch for, no?

Thus the old saying, "Where there's a will, there's a lawsuit...er...way." That's almost rather discouraging the way I see it, though. Like, a seeker can do the work diligently all their life but if that mysterious will never activates, they can just be poof, gone. Not very motivating, is it?

If a seeker has diligently done the work, they will not "just be poof, gone." Once something is internalized and Realized, nothing can take that away other than deliberate Intent to step off the path and ensuing neglect of the Other and the self with regard to evolution.

If you were to achieve total awareness and permanent gnosis with your Other, but had the misfortune to be struck on the head by a small comet and lose all memory, what you have already accomplished can't be taken away. It has already become a part of the living hologram. Under those circumstances, one of two things could happen. 1) You would transcend at the moment of mortal death rather than transmogrify; or 2) You would still transmogrify based on the actions of your Other.

The Other isn't prone to amnesia or dementia or traumatic brain injury, which is yet one more reason it is designed by default to be both within and without. To be absurdly simplistic for a moment, the Other is your spare set of keys in case you get locked out of yourself through illness, old age, or trauma. It can open the door even if you are unable, and for anyone who has *truly* done the work, it will. In that case, what occurs is actually a half-step between transmogrification and transcension.

Because the Other works in the movement of energy, it might not deem it necessary to reabsorb the entire physical body, leaving behind the mortal shell, but wholly taking the essence/identity/awareness of the

190

mortal self into itself just prior to the moment of physical death.

While transmogrification is the most mysterious and thorough method of attaining the immortal condition – only because it takes with it *all* the energy of the mortal self, including those aspects which comprised the organic form – it isn't always the most preferred, particularly by some who would be considered enlightened monks or shamans or other similarly evolved spirits. Many choose to live a complete and whole mortal life, up to and including the experience of "crossing over with awareness." They may choose to live to an uncomfortable old age so as to gain as much wisdom and insights into the universe as possible, doing so with the total understanding that the essence of who they are is not the vessel in which the essence walks around on Earth.

As the old saying goes, "You are not your body." For those who attain a much higher state of awareness and choose to remain among the living until their body can no longer sustain them, it is often observed by the immortals that they step out of the meat suit and into the Other instantly, and with absolute awareness of precisely what has occurred. The transition between mortal and immortal is seamless.

So to clarify, those rare few who have attained awareness aren't simply poof-gone even if the will never rises. There are many pathways to the bardo. Some are difficult to explain and even more difficult to comprehend because the concept itself has been programmed out of human beings in general. This is precisely why it is considered forbidden knowledge by the church, and considered insanity by the laws of man. You aren't "meant" to know these things, and that is no accident. It is how the powerful retain their power.

Can the Other Ever Betray You?

Can the Other betray you?
I ask this knowing full-well it is created out of unconditional love, and I know that it can't destroy you since you're its lifeline... except, at a certain point, you're not. When the twin starts dreaming you, and especially at a point when riding the ghost train[25] becomes a possibility, couldn't the twin be said to be a sovereign being, capable of sustaining itself without needing your help? Can there ever be a point at which the twin decides helping you is far less entertaining than roaming the sunken stars on colossal poetry arcs?

The connection you might be overlooking is that even though the twin can become autonomous, there is an underlying knowledge (certainty) that it is not whole until it conjoins with its mortal source.

> **The mortal self is the point of creation of the double, so the power of creation itself lies within the ironically mortal half of the immortal equation.**

While you might be marginally correct to say "...except, at a certain point, you're not," that would have to be completely internalized down to a quantum

---

[25] **Ghost Train**: a peculiar interaction between mortal self and immortal Other. Should the mortal fail to achieve transmogrification or transcendence, there is a theory that the highly-developed Other has the ability to step back inside the hologram of time to a point when the mortal self was still in the mother's womb. By entering the mortal self prior to birth, the Other is then "born" into the same body as the mortal self – the agenda being to enforce the mortal self's evolution by existing as the internal teacher. For anyone with an understanding of quantum mechanics, this is not so far-fetched, since time is not linear but actually a sphere, where all events are non-local. Put simply, the 'ghost train' runs back and forth on the same track until such time as the mortal self and the Other conjoin to create the singularity/totality of both.

level, which is a feat the Other can manage, but seldom one the mortal self can achieve. The Other would know it doesn't really need your help, but if it wants to know totality, it needs the components of the mortal self that created it in the first place (which, some say, are the very elements that make certain doubles "Creators"), and the only way to achieve Totality is with the conjoining of self/double – which is precisely why a sufficiently-evolved double will be compelled to manifest the ghost train indefinitely, or at least as long as there is some possibility that the mortal self will eventually transition into a full union with the Other itself.

Some immortals speculate that even though the Other can theoretically survive without conjoining to its mortal source, it gradually tends to weaken and might even run the risk of discorporating despite its own best intentions.

Can the double betray you? Not in the way you are suggesting, though it can walk away from you for long periods of "time" when you are off dallying and distracted in the dayshine world. It can even throw obstacles in your path in an attempt to derail you from whatever is distracting you, the agenda being to wake you up and get you back on the Way. Never forget: the Other is fighting for *their* immortality as well as yours, all paradoxes and irreducible conundrums notwithstanding.

The only way the Other could actually leave you would be if you walked away from the path altogether, stopped being a seeker, and became instead a flag-waving supporter of the consensual agreement, the local church, and the PTA. At that point, if the double realizes all hope is lost, they have the ability to fold their wings, turn to mist, and vanish from your life altogether.

At what point would that occur? Keep in mind that the Other has future-sight if it has become sufficiently evolved. If it can be perceived that the mortal self will never return to the path, will never achieve transmogrification or transcension, the Other further realizes that *it* will not achieve totality either. At such a point, the Other will either "give up the ghost" or sever the connection with the mortal self so as to maintain whatever individuation it had attained.

The Other can't betray you or leave you willy nilly. However, if *you* betray or Intentionally leave the Other, there are no guarantees. Be very clear on this: when I say "if you leave the Other" I am speaking of what would amount to walking away from a once-loved cabin in the woods, sealing it up, and then burning it to the ground. Only then would it be gone forever. I've seen seekers do that, at which point they can no longer be called seekers, just phantoms on the road to Extinction.

Would the twin not fight tooth claw and nail for its own survival if threatened by a stupid seeker? Perhaps take extreme lengths to wake up the mortal before it chose to abdicate the path altogether?

Absolutely. This can account for why some seekers might initially believe the twin has betrayed them or, in the words of a former apprentice who *did* return to the dayshine world, "My Other is just deliberately fucking with my life!"

That might be true.

When you give the twin carte blanche to "teach me and make me immortal" the twin takes that quite literally. However – and this is the darker side of that coin – the one thing you *can't* give your twin is your own free will. If the seeker is sufficiently stubborn (or "stupid" as you aptly put it), the Other doesn't have the ability to force its human source to stay on the path.

Seems to me any significantly evolved seeker would have a bit more than small trouble returning to the consensus. There really is a point of no return, is there not?

194

Yes, there is a point of no return, but that doesn't mean the seeker will be compelled to finish the journey into immortality even if they have crossed beyond that hypothetical point. It only means they will not be able to completely immerse themselves in the dayshine world. They will remain in a sort of limbo where they know (and cannot *un*know) too much to go back to a normal life. But at the same time they won't pursue the path either, usually having decided it's too hard, or not real, or some other reason concocted in their own mind as a form of justification.

If their Other is sufficiently advanced, there is a possibility it would invoke the ghost train when the mortal self came to the end of its life, but there is even a point where *that* is highly unlikely, such as...

It's been said that the future is always in flux, so even if the double can *see* the seeker headed in the direction of abandoning the path altogether, the double will fight until the *second* point along the way when there is no longer even the vaguest doubt about the impending outcome. This usually occurs when the seeker – often in a fit of rage or self-pity – commands the double to go away, be gone, go fuck yourself, leave me alone, hit the road, Jack, and don't you come back no more, no more!

At *that* point, the will of the seeker overshadows even the will of the Other. At *that* point, it's "Game over, man. Game over!" Such was the fate of my former apprentice. There was a time when she *could* have decided to return to the path, but chose instead to become the phantom she had, in truth, always been.

That's when the Other either severs all connection to the mortal self and chooses to exist as a sovereign entity without its totality, or it intentionally abandons its own cohesion and returns its energy and experiences to the dark sea of awareness.

The Process of Becoming

*The process of becoming
is the foundation of being. (MN)*

*I've read these words a dozen times and they keep
impacting me more and more every time I look at them.
There really is a process, even if it's only an
instantaneous transition from mortal to immortal, but the
twin is definitely the key, or else wouldn't it all just
dissipate into the universal stew, like a cup of water
being poured into the ocean? So if the twin is that 'thing'
holding the self together, then what is the twin and why
does it seem to be a stumbling block for some seekers?*

Ego and fear are at the core of why some resist the
idea of the Other. There is a tendency to see the twin as
separate from the Self, when it is more accurately a
reflection and projection of the self. It *is* the self in its
totality, especially when viewed from outside the limiting
confines of time.

The Other is the "Thing" that holds awareness intact
once the physical form is shed and the seeker becomes
pure energy. Words cannot really wrap around what the
Other *is*, except to say it is the vessel of one's immortal
awareness and the projection of one's immortal essence
beyond the event horizon of mortal death or in the
aftermath of transmogrification.

Why is it a stumbling block? Because the ego likes
to believe it is contained entirely within the mortal coil,
and any suggestions to the contrary instill fear and
loathing in every cell of one's humanform self-
importance.

Without the Other, yes it would be like pouring a
cup of water into an ocean. The Other is the binding
force – impervious to death and also impervious to the
ravages of time, because it is not a part of Time.

How would you describe "the process of becoming" with regard to achieving what you call the immortal condition? I've observed in your books that a lot of people want to do things their own way and you always encourage them, but I get the feeling there's something you're holding back.

From a purely rational perspective, the process is easy to describe but apparently quite difficult for many to comprehend. If forced to condense it down to steps, I would say it is this:

1. *Dream the Other.* This can take many forms – meditation, dreaming, longing, imagination, creativity in all its manifestations, following the muse, listening to the songs of your heart. I have described it in *Teachings of the Immortals* as "the ache/hurt/want/need." This is the quantifiable force that summons the Other and binds it into what might be perceived as an energy body. Prior to that, it exists as fragmented "feelings" or distant and vague longing for that "something missing" which most seekers experience from very early on in their journey, often as far back as early childhood.

2. *Nurture the other.* There are certain techniques for strengthening the Other in the beginning stages of the path, but as time wears on, you will experience precisely what you're saying – it will tend to come and go with regard to intensity and even frequency. The only way to combat that would be to find ways to keep it fresh and current.

Most seekers who eventually drop from the path or flit to a different flower are those who get bored and disillusioned when things start to require work as opposed to just happening naturally. Particularly in the early stages of the journey, the twin will often perform incredible displays of power, reminiscent in some ways of a hummingbird in spring doing aerial maneuvers that defy gravity in an attempt to attract a mate. But as with any relationship – and especially this one – it has to be kept vibrant and immediate, and how you do that will vary widely from one seeker to the next. Some may find that reading their own journals from a time when things were at a peak of excitement will help to rekindle the fires. Others might turn to favorite books or films that guided the journey at certain points along the way.

Even though it is advised to eliminate most routines, it is often helpful where the Other is concerned to engage in a practice of "talking" with them just prior to going to bed. Stand by a window and look out at the night. Allow your mind to drift toward gnosis. Converse with the Other as you would with a best friend, even a lover. Bring them to you.

If you are familiar with the process of automatic writing, sit at your computer, or with pen and paper, and ask the Other to speak to you. Don't try to make logical sense of the words as they come, just write them down and study them later. At first you might get only what seems to be gibberish, but gnosis is such that it seeks its own level as you practice it, as you find a frequency common to self and Other. Just be careful not to let your own internal dialog take over. Sneaky bastard that it is, it will try to trick you because that is what it is designed to do.

Form a fierce bond with the Other through visualization, gnosis and the relentless energy of Intent.

Above all, keep it focused and rooted in Unconditional Love.

3. *Think on this.* Consider the idea that the Other is like an indestructible element of "the cloud" into which you upload your awareness through the process of living. But far more than that, the Other is the energetic aspect of yourself who experiences what are commonly mislabeled as past lives or future lives. As such, the

Other is already infinite and eternal, but *only* if the seeker does the work of creating, nurturing and Dreaming the Other into a viable and powerful entity with a life (or thousands of lives) of their own.

The Other doesn't exist by default, as many religions like to teach with regard to the soul. Instead, it is built, strengthened and projected by the seeker's intent and – far more important – the seeker's unconditional love.

> *When you can come to me*
> *leaving no footprints in the snow*
> *Then and only then*
> *will it be time*
> *to end Time*
> *for all time.*

4. *You have to <u>be</u> immortal before you will know how to <u>become</u> immortal.* The Other is the answer to that riddle, in the sense that as the seeker looks through the eyes of the Other and begins to "remember the Other self," there is a moment of a quantum leap wherein the Other became/becomes autonomous, takes their first immortal breath, and begins Dreaming (teaching) the mortal self *how* to get to that moment of the quantum leap.

5. *You have to feel it.* If you don't have this intense love for the Other, then chances are you don't have the intense love for *yourself*, which is what ultimately enables you to transcend the command of the matrix which states, "All things die." With regard to "feeling" it, there's an entry in *Darker Teachings of the Immortals* that speaks to what that might look like:

> I once loved someone so much that I could
> not abide the thought of his death. Growing old.
> Wasting to the dust. Forever gone.

I schemed. I wept. I mourned him even though he was still alive. So young. Vital. Vibrant. Friend. Companion. Muse.

Knowing I could not *(would not, could not, would not)* live in a world where he did not exist, I took it upon myself to *Become* a thing capable of defeating Death itself. Not because I wanted to. Not because I even believed I could. But because *I had to.*

"For I am divided for love's sake, for the chance of union ." (Aleister Crowley)

Words are not capable of defining this kind of love. It is not rooted in some petty notion of sexual coupling. It is not about holding hands and walking into the sunset together. It is not brotherly or sisterly or husbandly or wifely.

It simply *is.* The awe one feels when the stars are falling in early autumn. The catch-in-the-throat when the moon rises huge and golden over a restless sea. The peace of knowing – without doubt – now he can never die.

It is the love that poets struggle to describe and inevitably fail. It is the love that forces us to do the impossible and the illegal and the insane and the incomprehensible, even when it has never been done before and all the world tells us we are fools to believe we will be The One.

It is the force that makes us immortal.

There is only this terrible ache that beats like a drum and calls itself Love, demanding to be acknowledged.

This is the Love that causes me to shake a fist at gods and demons, summoning the ability and the right to live forever. It is what gives us – any immortal who chooses it – the power to take a beloved by the hand and say to them, "Here, my friend. Come with me and let me show you what you can be. Don't be afraid. Breathe in the animus of life itself, the elixir of love, and fly free so that we may explore and experience the unknown now and forever."

There is no greater love than this.

Often it is the heartbreaks
that shape the Spirit
and redefine the heart itself.

Love is the foundation of immortal creation. Love is a quantifiable force - a power similar in nature to a bolt of lightning, possessing the ability to destroy and create in a single strike.

PART SIX
The Immortal Realm[26]

Here the abacus of time is broken.
Lanterns are keepers of souls,
crows the guardians
on the outskirts of Neverland.

———

Between Two Worlds
The duality of reference points

I was reading through Darker Teachings of the
Immortals and came across the section "Death is a
Position of the Assemblage Point." In it you state that, "It
could be observed in most ordinary humans that death
occurs when the assemblage point moves to a position
that is without reference points within the world of matter
and men. There is the perception of nothing, yet that very
nothing is a perception, which implies there is something
doing the perceiving."

———————————————

[26] **Immortal Realm**: *1. A state of mind but also a state of being. 2. A separate
reality which exists as a result of the seeker's own intent and will. 3. A quantum
other-world or alternate dimensional reality.* Shadowland is a concept which must
be sensed, felt and intuited so that it is created with sufficient strength to exist both
as a concept and as a separate reality capable of being inhabited. The transitioned
immortal may exist simultaneously in the ordinary world and in Shadowland. This
is the nature of immortal duality – bi-location of mind/body/spirit, the state of
mind which opens the door to all other-dimensional perceptions.

Perhaps I am mistaken, but I got the impression that "ordinary" humans who cross the threshold of death essentially obliviate, i.e., there is nothing left even to "perceive nothing." But the statement above would seem to contradict that.

This is one of those conundrums rooted solidly in duality – wherein two things exist simultaneously and in seeming contradiction to one another. In other words – it's both. And it's neither. When an ordinary human dies, the assemblage point shifts to such an extreme position that there are no reference points *other* than oblivion itself. But since oblivion is something that can be described and experienced, it qualifies as a valid position of the assemblage point.

However, the keyword in this discussion should perhaps be "cohesion." Those who transition and become immortal maintain their individuated cohesion even when the assemblage point shifts drastically to a point of no-reference. When that occurs, the reference point becomes the self and – more accurately – the Other. In an instant (no time at all), the cohesive awareness shifts from organic to inorganic, and a new series of reference points is created. This would naturally include those previously known in the world of matter and men, but also what might be termed more specialized reference points generally only available to the inorganics, the allies and the immortals.

The trick is learning to adapt to those new reference points and weave them into one's pre-existing awareness (what one brings over from their mortal life experience) without allowing the new reference points to become instruments of chaos and destruction. In other words, the trick is not to go mad when transitioning from one set of references to the next.

This is why I say seekers must build a new foundation during the process of being alive, so that when they do transition the experience is like stepping across a bottomless chasm... but the step is only a foot across rather than a mile-wide abyss. If the new reference points are perceived only as frightening or incomprehensible, madness is a strong possibility.

What, then, does a person perceive once they've moved the assemblage point to an immortal position?

An immortal's reference points would include whatever the individual had gained from the world of matter and men, *plus* what amounts to a *new* preceptor that becomes active once one passes through (or around) the state known as death. It's why many who have had near death experiences become "psychic" in the aftermath – essentially they bring back with them a minuscule bit of the immortal's perception.

How to describe that perception? Not really possible, anymore than trying to describe an orgasm to a can of beans. In certain literature, immortals might have abilities they didn't have as mortals. Some can read thoughts. Others can heal or cause physical distress to others. Others may absorb knowledge directly from the fabric of the universe. Still others might be able to fly or discorporate altogether. All of these things (and so many more that cannot even be captured with words) are just expanded positions of the assemblage point.

How does an immortal actually perceive? Humans perceive with the five senses and sometimes intuition if they allow themselves to do so. The immortal is not necessarily tied to a physical body, correct? Does he or she have to project a physical body to, say, smell a rose?

Immortals perceive directly. An immortal would *become* the essence of the rose and therefore would know it intimately, from the inside out, so to speak. By the same token, most immortals who have adjusted to their newly acquired perceptions would tend to perceive from a position outside of time. For example, if a book were lying in front of an immortal, but they hadn't yet read it, they could read it "instantaneously" (to ordinary perceptions) by projecting awareness into a future point in time (a new reference point), wherein they *had* read the book. Then, when returning to whatever point in time they inhabited when the book was just lying on the table, they would have total knowledge of it (having read it in the future). Much simplified, but essentially accurate.

Immortals recognize the first and most important agreement of the new perception – that time is indeed the first fundamental lie. Once free of time – truly free and not just as an intellectual mortal dalliance – the immortal is also freed to navigate instantaneously between Then and Now, Past and Present, Here and There. So... this brings up the four agreements of the immortal condition.

1. Time is the first fundamental lie, the hag-bride of Death.

2. My foundation is malleable rock. It is built on the knowledge that it exists (even when I cannot *see* it directly), and therefore it is built on the knowledge that I am forever building and extending it from one non-moment to the infinite next.

3. Evolution is an ongoing process. It does not stop when I "die" or when I am re-born as an immortal. Each ending is the new beginning.

4. Life is a position of the assemblage point, counterpoint to Death. Therein lies the secret to living forever, the key to getting out of life *alive.*

The Dark Side of the Night Light

Mikal, as I reread your books again, I am keenly aware of the many difficulties and dangers of immortality that you write about. You speak of the sometimes incredible loneliness of immortality, of losing so many people that you love, of sometimes damning your personal creator for making you immortal, of the real dangers of not being totally prepared before you transmogrify and ending up in a nowhere land and going mad. I have no problem with that. But what about the positive side? Yes, you never die, I know, but what else? You can go anywhere in any time and appear as anything you choose, what you can do is only limited by your imagination. I have no problem understanding loneliness, losing loved ones etc, but lately I have difficulty imagining the endless realm of possibilities as an immortal.

I don't write as much about the "endless realm of possibilities as an immortal" because the possibilities truly are endless, and what calls to me might have little or no interest to anyone else. It becomes a case of finding one's own unique frequency as an immortal, following not only your heart but also your predilections – which might change dramatically when you transition from organic to inorganic.

Also, it's one of those funny little facts that if I *did* talk about it, chances are no one would believe me anyway. I could tell you, for example, what a sunset and simultaneous moonrise is like on Eridani Prime, but most would take my words as a faltering attempt at fiction or, at best, bad poetry.

What I can say with certainty is that everyone who makes the leap across the mortal abyss usually sits on the edge of that abyss for a century or two, feet dangling over the side, with an expression of slack-jawed amazement, amusement, terror, and what might be best called astonishment that one hadn't seen it all along.

Seen what? The answer. What answer? All of them. And yet... all the answers in all the worlds mean nothing without perspective, and immorality is the venue in which one gains that perspective... which takes a lifetime or 10, and what *is* a lifetime (or 10) to an immortal?

Also, when you transmogrify you join up with your twin and the two of you become one, so to speak. But then what of love and companionship? Do you still wish to express love to another or are you complete unto yourself?

I could say that when you conjoin with your Other, you inhabit the totality of yourself, bringing together under one assemblage point all memories of all so-called past lives or future lives or parallel lives... the experiences amassed by the Other. But because there *is* a human tendency to need (or at least want) juxtaposition, it is entirely possible (and quite common) for the self and the Other to take separate forms so as to interact in a manner more familiar to the Self.

Eventually most choose the united assemblage point of totality, but there are no rules and no wrong answers. Energy can take any form or more than one form, simultaneously. This is why I have often said that Man has a dual assemblage point – that of the mortal self, and that of the immortal Other.

"For the sake of love, I am divided." (Aleister Crowley)

You once described in detail the agony you went through as a result of losing cohesive awareness and becoming sort of a non-entity – just disembodied, impersonal awareness. Your description made a deep impact on me. Did this experience happen when you transmogrified and you weren't sufficiently prepared and so you had to claw your way back from that nowhere land, or was this something you tried after you had transmogrified

I believe you are referring to "the land of the sentient dead." I've had several encounters with that state of being. As a mortal, it can be virtually impossible to pull oneself up out of that comforting embrace. As an immortal, it is equally difficult, but "time" is on one's side... until it isn't. It is possible to become trapped in that state forever, and some immortals do. Some even choose it as an alternative to the darker aspects of immortality (loneliness being first and foremost). Most who do choose it as a permanent "solution" are those I would categorize as being energetically transmogrified, but spiritually still all too human.

For myself, my journeys into the land of the sentient dead were predicated by curiosity. What's the point of being immortal if one can't experience all there is to experience? Rather like going to Disneyland and failing to go on Pirates of the Caribbean.

Now, having been-there-done-that, it is not something I would consciously choose to do again.

Why can't we remember our past lives, and what are past lives?

The Other isn't confined by space or time, so it is free to experience what you think of as "past lives" throughout the space/time continuum. It can localize in ancient Greece or in the throne room of the elders on Sirius IX.

You actually *can* remember certain aspects of what you think of as past lives – usually through a strong connection to silent knowing (gnosis), but also sometimes in Dreaming or deep-trance meditation. Many times you will catch a glimpse of something, at which point the key becomes one of tracing the "download" that generally accompanies such visionary experiences.

You'll usually find that these "past lives" don't really track from point of birth to point of death, but instead may revolve around specific short-term events. For example, you might only remember standing on a barren and frozen mountaintop, knowing you have achieved your goal of climbing the mountain, but also knowing you will not survive to ever go home again. What is the lesson here? How does this align with your everyday life in the Now?

Because the Other isn't restricted by normal human rules, they might enter into such a lifetime for what – to human perceptions – would only consist of a few days or weeks. But if the Other considers such an experience worthy of undertaking, it's a certainty that there is something for the mortal self to learn.

Are there any specific techniques for remembering past lives?

Although many a new age guru has made his fortune attempting to proffer such techniques, most are little more than mind games the seeker is being encouraged to play on herself as a means to stroke the guru's ego and load his wallet.

In actuality, the only *real* technique I know of is the work of the path itself. Any actual "past life memories" might be behind a veil through which the mortal self can't always see, but which is always transparent and accessible to the Other.

Aside from that, if you find yourself haunted or taunted by something in particular – an unreasonable fear of heights, for example, or an unreasonable attraction to the sea, focus your meditations and gnosis in that direction. Quite often, a single "glimmer" of a memory is a porthole that can be opened onto an entire vista.

Does Physical Immortality Exist?

In most cases, physical immortality is little more than longevity, and turns out to be a dangerous deterrent to transmogrification because the mind/body/spirit is misled by what they *think* is immortality to such an extent that they feel no need to further their evolution beyond that point.

As to how transformation (so-called physical immortality) occurs, or why it is a goal for some...

Many (most) are conditioned to truly believe they *are* their body, and that if they can preserve the structure, the essence will continue to inhabit the structure. There are multiple problems with that, not the least of which has to do with brain capacity and might be boiled down to a major storage problem.

If you think of the brain as the humanform computer, it is a finite item and can only hold so much data before it will begin to dump or fail to upload additional information once its memory is full. From a very narrow perspective, this is why a lot of people develop memory loss and dementia – when the brain reaches its capacity, the mind (the search function) can no longer operate efficiently, and a vast amount of data is either shredded or never stored in the first place. Clearly it is more complicated than that, but unless a deeper understanding is sought, that is sufficient to grasp the gist of the problem.

Where transformation is concerned, it increases the ability of the body to withstand the elements of time, but the brain isn't always completely on board with that. As a result, a lot of "physical immortals" might fare quite well for a century or two, but eventually they become like a lost child at an amusement park.

Everything is bright and shiny and looks like loads of fun, but without reference points – which begin to erode due to those same elements of time – there can be an increasing lack of connectivity to the world at large, which often resembles paranoia, fear, and a very dark state of depression.

In addition, once an individual has become transformed (as opposed to transmogrified or transcended), most of the motivation to take it to the *next* level is lost. Worse, assuming this individual might have been a seeker prior to their transformation, they would have to essentially start over from Square One, eliminating the programs and belief systems that have accumulated since attaining "physical immortality."

The fact that someone might achieve that state doesn't prevent old programs from coming back, or new ones from forming. This is why I stress that this is an ongoing process, and an open-ended evolution. There is no beginning, middle or end. There is only the constant awareness that nothing in this world is truly static, not even liquid nitrogen. Nothing can stop time except to be outside of it altogether, and as long as there is a physical body (whether mortal or immortal), it is subject to at least some of the rules of the consensual world.

To give you a more direct answer to your direct question, most true seekers really don't pine after physical immortality. However, there are circumstances under which transformation can occur spontaneously (just as transmogrification can occur spontaneously – though it's rare in *any* circumstance). If a seeker suddenly finds himself in a seemingly "immortal" physical body, the very best thing he could do would be to invoke the Other and remind them that they, too, are now anchored to the foundation of the organic world.

The bottom of the bottom line is simply that physical immortality comes with certain dire consequences, not the least of which is that it can and usually does bind the Other to the mortal self rather than freeing the mortal self to transmogrify/transcend and bind to the Other. To better visualize the situation, would you pour the contents of a bottle of Petrus 1989 into a leaky paper cup? Even so-called physical immortals are vulnerable to destruction and final death, and if your Other happens to be anchored to the physical body, they won't be able to protect you when a comet hits the earth or the sun goes nova or the next wave of Crusaders separate your head from your neck or burn your "immortal" body at a Klan rally.

Physical immortality is an illusion from a truly immortal perspective. It is speculated that within the next 25-30 years it will be possible for humans to experience extreme longevity which, you may rest assured, will be marketed as "virtual immortality." And who's to say? Maybe it will be. But I am willing to predict that the devil is in the details, and even altering the genetic material won't make anyone immortal anymore than a facelift will make anyone young again. Illusions are the foundation of the global economy and the Achilles heel of the human animal.

As with everything, physical immortality comes with a long list of potential consequences. It might be useful as a stop-gap measure – buying the seeker more time in which to attain the immortal condition through transmogrification – but only for the most determined and disciplined seekers who recognize the inherent dangers before inserting foot into trap.

The Truth About Transmogrification

What happens if your body does not die, but you transmogrify?

That's more or less the entire point of transmogrification – it allows the seeker to become immortal without passing through Death. Even though transcension achieves the same end result, there is some argument amongst immortals as to whether transcension *might* have the side effect of robbing a certain amount of energy from the totality. There is no definitive proof one way or the other, but it is generally believed that transmogrification enables the seeker to take every microgram of energy with him, including whatever memory or experience might be stored in the subatomic structure of the body itself.

Does your body suddenly change to a young, healthy, and whole version of yourself? And if so, how do you explain that to those who know you?

Since the transmogrified individual doesn't exist in a physical body, but in a *meta*-physical body, it can appear as anything you choose. If you want to be 25 and female, it's a matter of learning to focus on that paradigm. Most times, a newly-transmogrified individual will appear as they did in life. It depends marginally on how you *see* yourself beyond your physical form. Once one becomes immortal, it's easy enough to learn to navigate and quickly becomes second nature unless the individual is extremely hung up on the idea of a *physical* body. If that's the case, though, chances are they never would transmogrify in the first place.

As for people you've known in your mortal lifetime, this is one reason a lot of seekers choose a solitary path and strive to be unknown. While it is possible for a transmogrified individual to maintain certain human contacts (by essentially learning to project the expected bodily image to acquaintances) it is a chore that tends to lose its allure quicker than you might think.

In many ways, an evolved/transmogrified individual is as different from a human as a human is different from an ape. There are similarities and even certain connections (mostly emotional) but once you attain your totality, it becomes much more difficult (and at the same time much easier) to maintain a facade of a normal human life. Some do it for awhile, then quietly disappear, often using the excuse that they are moving to Outer Mongolia.

Are you permanently barred from interacting in this world from then on?

Not at all. Who would bar you? It merely becomes a question of whether or not the masks you would have to wear are worth the effort of putting them on every day.

How do you get a driver's license if you're immortal? Sooner or later they are going to notice your birth date doesn't match your appearance.

Immortals who choose to live a human-style life know the ins and outs of assuming an identity that is feasible. It might surprise you that the sinister "they" usually don't notice much of anything at all. The authorities only care if your taxes are paid or that the photo on the driver's license more or less matches the mug shot if one happens to get arrested. For the most part, immortals are fairly savvy and tend to avoid entanglements with authority.

If your twin is the opposite gender, which one do you become if you transmogrify?

Again, whatever you choose. Keep in mind that the twin can be opposite gender today and same gender tomorrow, and is always what you *need* them to be, even if not always what you might *want* them to be. In most cases, the transmogrified individual takes on the attributes of the Other for the simple reason that the Other is the representation of the perfected Self. Gender is a humanform issue.

It's been said that a seeker who transmogrifies can either unite wholly with the Other to become a single entity, or they might choose for whatever reason to maintain the illusion(?) of two separate beings. What's the truth behind that?

You can do/be whatever you want if you successfully transmogrify. *There are no limitations.* If you choose to remain as "two," you are *still* actually One. If you wanted to maintain the illusion of separateness, you might split your awareness between the "two" but in the grand scheme of it all, you can't tickle yourself.

You are The One.

Fear of Failure or Fear of Success?

I know people are walking the tightrope between crazy and crazier, but what is it about the subject of immortality that sends people over the edge completely?

It would take an entire book just to touch the surface of that question, but the core problem is that humans have been taught to fear the things they don't understand, as well as to accept the word of learned men with letters after their names, even when those learned men prove themselves to be fools a thousand times over.

Fear. But why? It goes something like this...

The mortal human program, which is indirectly full of religious dogma at the core level, whether anyone *sees* it or not, is such that the idea of living forever in a human/organic body has been denigrated to such a degree that it comes with an entire plethora of dark images and potential horrors. "Sure, kid, you can live forever, but your body will grow old and decrepit, and that portrait in the attic ain't gonna do you any good when your organs fall out your backside and your brain starts to mummify, and you're left crawling around on the floor of some dank basement like a zombie. It ain't *natural*, kid! Just ain't right, and God wouldn't approve and why are you messin' with things you ain't got no business messin' with? Eat your cereal and read your Bible and get with the program and quit talkin' about this stuff before somebody hears you and ships you off to Facebook jail or worse!"

Fear.

The thing about fear is that it often has some basis in reality. I do not personally promote the idea of "transformation" even though it does not come with the manifestations of the fears mentioned above. It is simply not particularly practical as a long-term solution because physical immortality would nonetheless leave one open to accident or global obliteration. I was recently having a discussion with an advanced apprentice about this very thing, because it seems that several writers are promoting the idea of "physical immortality" as a viable and permanent solution to death.

I would consider that myopic at best, but whenever my apprentice attempts to bring forth the idea of transmogrification or transcension, she is met with fear, anger and even threats on occasion. Again... *why*? Undoubtedly it is because transmogrification or transcension require a significant amount of work, whereas this idea of physical immortality is often

216

presented as a matter of bizarre dietary choices, or what deity one might pray to for longevity, or – worse – some technological upload of one's awareness into what would amount to a simulation, more commonly known as the "singularity."

I am not suggesting that these options are unreasonable. Be as healthy as you can be – just don't expect good health to equal immortality anymore than 20/20 vision would give you psychic insight. The two might *seem* related, but really aren't.

What you eat or don't eat won't make you immortal. Such choices *might* lengthen or shorten your mortal life to some extent, but there are no supplements or fad diets or peculiar fruit smoothies that will infuse your body with the elixir of eternal life. Remember, you are not your body.

Until fairly recently I had a friend with whom I could talk about everything from hauntings to aliens. But when I asked him his thoughts on immortality, he found reasons to avoid talking to me at all. He said he didn't think we had any business messing around with the natural order of life and death.

His comments sound very much like the ingrained belief that humans have no business meddling in the affairs of the gods. But... *what* gods? Most never get as far as asking that question because even those who would consider themselves to be atheists are too busy cowering in terror from those same nonexistent deities.

As a brief aside for purposes of clarity, the thing about being an atheist is that it actually requires a paradoxical acknowledgement that there is or might be a god (or gods) in whom the atheist refuses to believe. Convoluted logic, but when really examined, it's often present – particularly in the case of militant atheists who wave their antithesis beliefs around like any militant Christian. It's a belief system, often ingrained in the mind since early childhood, just by virtue of living among humans who believe or disbelieve in some deity who hands out punishment for anyone who would dare to meddle in their affairs.

Obviously this is a very hidden subliminal programming to anyone whose eyes are otherwise open, but I've seen it kick in even among the most devout atheists who would claim they have no fear of divine retribution... right up to the point where I say to them, "How would you like to live forever?" That's when the trouble starts, because it slams up against a long-buried program that is more of a social/cultural conditioning than any personal belief. It might even be part of the operating system that makes one human – what amounts to a shared mainframe operating in the background – not because it is right or good, but because it has evolved from ancient times. Part of the reptilian brain more than any rational or reasonable installation.

So what is that scares people so much about this path in particular? Is it fear of failure or fear of success?

Fear of success is a tremendous part of the equation. If one succeeds in becoming immortal, it comes with a much greater responsibility than if one sees the exit sign at the end of the tunnel and perceives life to be finite.

The mindset of a mortal who has accepted their fate is vastly different than the mindset of a mortal who has made the commitment to break the chains of their programming. So whether one fears success or failure, fear is always at the heart of why immortality is such a threat to a system that depends on mentally and spiritually enslaved mortals to keep the wheels turning.

Making the Unreal Estate Real

There aren't any limits to how big or detailed your Shadowland might be, yes? So I might as well set my imagination free and design it from the largest continent to the smallest rock on a seashore, from the lowest tree in the forest to highest mountaintop. You can make it with any laws of physics or rules (or lack of rules) you see fit?

You don't personally have to create every rock and every grain of sand. You are the visionary. Energy is the creator. If you envision a jagged shoreline with a crescent moon hanging low over the dark waters, your creative spirit fills in the gaps. The beach will have sand because beaches tend to do that. The mountains will have caves and crannies because mountains tend to do that. The castles may be shiny and new or old and mysterious – because *that* is where *your* creative energy takes over and follows your predilections.

Even so, you don't have to create every stone in the castle walls or know the internal biology of a dog should you want one at your side. The natural order follows your vision whether you know how it all works or not.

The Ghost Train
...and those pesky memories that never happened

What about people who are "born double" like the nagual man or woman[27]? Their Other isn't trapped in the mortal construct, right? Or is it and the Other and the mortal have to work together to transcend the mortal shell?

Completely different kettle of kettlefish. Those who are born double are often the result of having ridden the ghost train at least once – a highly-developed Other essentially stepping back into the mortal's life as what amounts to a do-over. That's a much-simplified explanation, but in such cases, the Other isn't trapped, but acting of its own free will in an attempt to serve as guide and mentor to a seeker who had come very close to transmogrification or transcension, but lost their will somewhere in the chaos of transforming.

How would one know one is riding the ghost train?

There are several clues. The first would be if you discover that you *were* "born double" – usually something that can best be validated by an acknowledged seer. That doesn't automatically mean you've had a trip on the ghost train, but it is highly likely. Another clue would be extreme frequency of déjà vu. I'm not talking about the occasional glimpse of déjà vu, but the extended variety when you would be able to tell a friend what lies around the next corner in a city you've never visited, or what the random lady in the crowd who pauses to ask you a question is going to say.

---

[27] **Nagual Man/Woman:** From the works of Carlos Castaneda and other traditional shamanism, a nagual is someone born with four compartments of energy rather than the traditional two compartments.. Many seers interpret this as evidence that the Nagual being comes into the world with their double already fully formed.

This also gives credence to the theory that time is a self-replicating loop – that even if the universe breathes in and breathes out (the big bang/big collapse) it isn't a *new* universe each time, but the old one reassembling itself on a repeating loop. The same people will be in the same place, and will say and do the same things... over and over until the end of the first fundamental lie.

It has been argued among mortals and immortals alike that there might be minute discrepancies between one's initial mortal life, and any subsequent manifestations that occur as a result of the Other facilitating a time loop.

A relatively high percentage of seekers report something generally called "memories that never happened." The seeker knows they went to a Halloween party with friends and that they had chosen a group costume theme of characters from *The Wizard of Oz.* This would be the "real" memory, perhaps something from last year or ten years in the past – something that can be validated by others who participated in the memory, or even by photographs and recordings. But in the memory that never happened (which has *all* the characteristics of any *real* memory), it was a Christmas party at a local church with the same group of friends and all were wearing reindeer antlers.

The seeker feels/*knows* this *also* happened, but cannot place it in real time, nor can it be independently validated. Occasionally – *rarely* – perhaps one of their friends might have a quasi-memory of the Christmas party, but dismissed it as a dream. Most of the time, as with all things on this journey, the seeker finds himself alone and must contemplate certain questions which are going to arise despite one's best efforts to dispel them.

Has my last blue marble rolled under the fridge, lost forever lost?

Am I really in padded room at the edge of the forest, watching Little Red Riding Hood follow Hansel and

Gretel into the Wicked Witch's castle while flying monkeys circle overhead?

Why would I go to a church Christmas party when the few friends I have are all pagan or agnostics?

Where are we going and why am I in this handbasket?

In the big picture, does it matter? It might be altogether irrelevant to the outcome, or perhaps it is/was a crossroads that might enable a different outcome.

Meaning?

Meaning that if it's a Halloween party in your *real-time* memory, perhaps something happened there that will influence some decision or course of action that will lead to transmogrification rather than the mortal death that created a need for the Other to invoke the ghost train in the first place. You might never know *what* that event was – maybe something someone said in passing that nonetheless made a deep impact crater in your brain. Or maybe the event *can* be recalled, such as a face to face encounter with your Other, even if you probably didn't recognize them as such at the time.

> **Memories that never happened are energetic intersections connecting your mortal existence to your immortal transformation – bridges between what "Fate" laid out for you, and how that fate might be altered.**

Seldom if ever are memories that never happened insignificant anomalies, but when traced through meditation, dreaming, and gnosis, often lead to discoveries that might require months or even years of ongoing contemplation in order to be fully understood.

As an aside, this is one more reason seekers are encouraged to keep a journal of anomalous events, for even though they might not make sense when they occur, it is widely observed that they are playing a profound role in the seeker's road to immortality itself. When you are in the midst of your darkest night of the soul, often your journal is the only source of light to bring you back to yourself.

Of course, the subject of memories that never happened is another entire issue for another loop on the merry-go-down, but it can't be ignored when considering the ghost train. And there rises another clue. Those who were born double the *first* time around (was there a first time?) will be born double *every* time. So again, an irreducible conundrum that simply has to be pondered from a position of *Now what?*

When all is said and done, wouldn't it be indistinguishable from a straight-up transmogrification, since reality is malleable and holographic? Technically, aren't we all riding the ghost train if we succeed?

Only if there is truth to the theory I was postulating in the paragraphs above. Even those who are born double still have to do the work that would create/manifest their Other in a sufficiently evolved state that they would have the power and *ability* to step back in "time" and re-enter the mortal self prior to its first screeching cry into the darkness.

I've known a few so-called naguals or double beings who believe they are somehow special or blessed. But as Della Van Hise pointed out in one of her books[28], it may well be that double-beings are the ironically fortunate fuck-ups of the seekers who didn't get it right the first time around, but who at least reached a point where their Other can put in for a re-do on behalf of the mortal self. The movie ended. The ending was sad. The Other didn't like how it ended, so they quickly rewrite the

---

[28] *Questions Along the Way: Conversations With a Quantum Shaman*; page 159 in the trade paperback edition.

script and jump into the main character's body so as to better determine and direct the outcome. Dark truth: sometimes it takes more than once.

Here's another one to twist your tweeter. If there *is* truth to the theory of the big bang/big collapse, then it could be said that all creatures are immortal, at least in the sense that they will live (and die) again... and again... and again. Personally I don't subscribe to that idea. The whole purpose of what I teach is the ability to extend, expand, and manifest awareness *outside* the traditional boundaries of space/time and quantum loopiness.

> **The Immortal Realm is the universe *you* create, not the one created for you by default.**

Knowing time *is* a fundamental lie gives the seeker the ability to manipulate it. This manipulation is best accomplished through the Other due to the Other's ability to move *outside* of time – in this case on the "ghost train." The mortal seeker *can* learn to manipulate time to a degree; however the amount of energy and "time" required to manipulate "time" is a factor to be seriously considered from the mortal perspective, but is irrelevant from the immortal point of view.

Immortals have all the time in the worlds to manipulate "time." Mortals simply... *don't*.

RTFM
(Read the Fucking Manual)

Being immortal doesn't come with an owner's manual, nor does it make you automatically smart or graceful. I once knew of a man who had transmogrified but couldn't wrap his mind around it in the early phases. So he kept doing silly things in an attempt to prove it to himself. Jumped in front of a car. Impact should have killed him, but he only suffered a few broken bones that weren't really bones at all, so he mended almost as soon as he stood up from his self-imposed ordeal.

Unconvinced still, he intentionally insulted a very large man on the wrong side of the tracks and got himself knifed. Again, the wounds should have been fatal, but because he was no longer in a physical body, he healed almost instantly. Idiot that he was, he told himself it was all a delusion. Surely he must be dreaming. Certainly no creature was *really* immortal.

So he went out to the train tracks at dusk and stood there staring at an approaching freight hauler that couldn't possibly stop in time. Prepared to meet his maker, he spread his arms outward (so the story goes) and the train hit him full-chest at full throttle...

He "came to" in the engineer's cabin, looking over at the driver of the train. To his surprise, the man looked to be an identical twin who was scowling at him with disdain and a look that said, "*Really?*"

When the transmogrified man started to speak, the engineer said only one word. "Asshole." Then on second thought, he added, "You've been driving the fucking train all along. You can either keep running over yourself or you can get out of your own way. I'm not going to save you again." And with that, the engineer vanished into thin air, leaving the astonished asshole in charge of his own fate and the locomotive that was plunging onward into the dark.

Is it a true story? Who's to say? The newly transmogrified are sometimes like infants in a weapons store. Lots to get into.

Is There A Right Time?

In "The Vampire Lestat", Marius tells Lestat that to endure immortality one "should have had some lifetime before you make them; and never, never make one as young as Armand."

Does this concept have some basis in reality? I'm very young and yet I feel like I could transmogrify today and would be just fine without much experience in "the real world". Could transmogrifying at an early age have its drawbacks?

This is one of those questions that has to be considered on an individual basis. *Generally* speaking, I would not "turn" anyone under the age of 28-30 because the brain/mind is still in the formative stages even into the mid-20s. That aside, because of cultural programming, *most* individuals under the age of 30 are not sufficiently mature to handle daily life, let alone *eternal* life. That isn't just Mikal being an Olde Fart. It is a conclusion based on many lifetimes of observation, and subject to change based on the veracity of each individual I encounter.

I have known a few who transmogrified or transcended at an earlier age (the youngest was 14, the others anywhere from 18-22), and the results were questionable at best. The 14-year-old was trapped in a perpetual state of puberty (a male) and even though he now inhabited an energy body, his mental status was such that every thought involved sex or sports competition. Tedious enough for a mortal. Virtually intolerable for an immortal.

I should point out that this young man had been seriously injured in an accident, but an immortal who had intended to be his mentor took it upon himself to connect with the injured boy through Dreaming, and began instructing him as much as possible under the circumstances (medically-induced coma). When the boy crossed over he did manage to transcend with the monumental effort of his mentor, but even though the boy had possessed a rudimentary proclivity common to seekers, he simply didn't have the life experience to make the leap from mortal to immortal emotionally and spiritually.

There is no happy or sad ending to this story. His mentor continues to work with him, but the boy is often sullen, disenfranchised, and suffering from teen angst even though he would biologically now be around 35. Developmentally arrested would be one way of putting it, though even that doesn't entirely cover it. No one's fault – neither the boy's nor his mentor's. It is simply a biological fact that the brain/mind doesn't mature as rapidly as the body, and the gap between the two can be catastrophic.

As for others I've known, the major difficulties they face involve what I can only describe as "immortal arrogance" – common among the newly transitioned, particularly those who transmogrified or transcended at a very young age. It boils down to thinking they know everything when in reality they know nothing and run the high risk of exposing themselves *and* their mentors out of self-importance alone. I could tell you horror stories... but as it's nowhere near Halloween, I shall refrain. Suffice to say, there are obviously exceptions to these dark tales, but they are also rare.

Occasionally someone with absolutely *no* experience as a seeker and *no* mentor will transcend or transmogrify for no reason anyone can logically determine. They are either terrified or convinced they are now on a par with Superman, and either manifestation comes with potentially tragic consequences.

For those with an interest in fictional accounts, there's an episode of an old television series called *Kindred: The Embraced* wherein a young man is turned against his will and with no knowledge of what is happening to him. Despite the predictable drama, it's nonetheless an interesting look at what can happen when an individual isn't prepared for the massive shifts of perception that accompany the movement of awareness from organic to inorganic. I seem to recall the episode was titled *Nightstalker*.

To answer your question, I've also known a few who have been "doing the work" since they first reared up on their hind legs, and those are the ones who might stand a chance at eternal life were they to transcend or transmogrify at an earlier age. The trick, regardless of age, is eliminating the programming that is put onto all human beings from long before the moment of conception.

For the longest time I've been operating under the assumption that upon transmogrification, the feeling would be like waking up from a dream. It would be as if you were suffering from amnesia your whole life and then suddenly it all came back to you in a flash, or if you came back from a DMT trip (with all your immortal friends asking you how it went). Having read some newer posts, specifically the one where immature young immortals are mentioned, I have reason to doubt this. I'd like an official confirmation.

Most "immature young immortals" never really did the work of dismantling their belief systems, so they transition in the same state they occupied as humans. Even those who might be classified as rebels or rogues are often little more than "contraries" – those who go against the grain just for the sake of going against the grain, but without necessarily understanding the underlying *reasons* for their own actions.

There are no guidelines for what it's like when transitioning from human to immortal. No two individuals ever tell the same story where that's concerned.

It's not the state of being (immortality) that requires experience to navigate it. It's your humanform life. The common denominator between most failed attempts at transmogrification resides in the fact that if the belief systems of the humanform remain intact after transmogrification or transcension, the individual is going to be a stranger in a strange land. They won't speak the language or understand the rules (because there really aren't any rules, and getting *that* through one's head is like teaching advanced calculus to a kindergartner without the foundation of general math.)

Too many who come to me for guidance are always looking for shortcuts. "How long is this gonna take?" "When do I get my super powers?" "Why can't you just turn me, Mikal?" All of those questions only indicate a total disregard for the work. Some can overcome themselves. Most can't.

Isn't there some inherent order to the universe that would prevent somebody who is clearly not ready from transmogrification?

Inherent order in the universe? Surely you jest. Think about nature. It allows species to inbreed to the point of extinction. It allows entire galaxies to collide, destroying countless billions of entire civilizations. It allows horrendous mutations that serve no real purpose. It serves up viruses and for... *what?* Some might argue that it is thinning the herd, but if that *is* what's happening, then it is directly attributable to Man and not really to Nature at all.

Overpopulation and under-education will always equal disaster. But that aside, to think there is an "inherent order" is to indirectly credit the universe with some manner of sentience – someone or something directing traffic and deciding who or who isn't "ready".

Nature might occasionally *appear* to be sentient or wise, and is often called "Mother Nature" as if it is a living being, but the darker reality is that this is just Man's attempt to create order out of the chaos, and to assign meaning where there really is none. Not something most would want to believe or even consider. Perhaps one gives up his belief in God, but transfers responsibility over to Nature. Still the same ugly pickle he's in, he's just renamed it in an attempt to make it more palatable.

What *really* determines when one is ready is when one simple does it. Usually if one *can* do it, one is ready. There are obviously exceptions, often the case of intervention such as what I described above re the 14-year-old boy. Left to his own devices, he never would have made the leap. So there are reasons immortals don't run helter-skelter through the night turning any pretty face that crosses their path. Fortunately, that's just Hollywood.

> **And though I've said it countless times, I will repeat it once again for anyone who was texting in class.** *No one can "turn" you but you. Your mentors can give you the key to the door, but you are the only one who can use that key to turn the lock.*

Here it is perpetual dusk,
forever autumn,
promise of winds and winters.
Time was hanged
for treason.

PART SEVEN
The Seekers Speak

It seems appropriate to give some attention to those who have walked this path for a considerable length of time. Often it is the perceptions of advanced seekers that stir the imagination and pique the wonder of the immortals themselves.

———

Allowing the Impossible

The question was recently raised, "Why do I seem to be unable to make direct contact with my Other?" One of my long-time apprentices responded with what I consider to be not only a valid explanation, but also a powerful lesson in allowing the impossible – a topic that merits continuous investigation.

~

One of the main things that drew me to this path and to Mikal in particular was the poetic angst that resides in all of us who have been on this journey for any length of time. Whenever I write poetry or scribble in my journal, it's almost always to or about my Other. I was recently having some stray thoughts about my own weird and twisted history, and how I've actually encountered my Other in the flesh more than once. Oh, he's still like an indefinable sprite, coming close but never allowing himself to be captured, never allowing that frenzied consummation which would undoubtedly result in my mortal death or instantaneous transmogrification (ready or not).

I sometimes wonder if the reason most seekers never meet their Other in the flesh is because they are pre-

programmed to believe they never will. We're conditioned to think of such things as dreams or daydreams, fantasies kids have like invisible friends. But somewhere along the way I fell thru the crack between the worlds, probably because I didn't have a lot of adult supervision as a child, and so my programming was sorely lacking in a lot of ways (which I personally consider to be a good thing!).

What I'm trying to say is that I never _didn't_ believe my Other was real – flesh and bone, and someone I would eventually meet. This goes back as far as I can remember. The Other has taken many forms in my mind, many different manifestations, but always the same foundational structure. Call it a certain type if you want. Tall. Dark. Handsome. Mysterious. Dangerous. Cunning. Brilliant. Sexual. Immortal.

I never thought he was a fantasy or an invisible friend. I truly _believed_ he was real and – later in life after I'd been conditioned through society to question my belief – I came to a point where I realized I had to _allow_ myself to not only go back to that belief in the physicality of him, but to also begin summoning him to "Come find me" with all the energy and longing I could muster – what Mikal has referred to as the ache/hurt/want/need all seekers feel, and is actually the catalyst that brings us to this path in whatever passes for the "beginning."

To my surprise – a shock so deep it almost physically destroyed me – one day he showed up. Nope, he didn't announce who or what he was. And so I was torn between certainty and suspicion, even though deep down I knew this was the manifestation of the magic I had spent a lifetime cultivating. The silly spells I had done over the years. The poetry I had written and cast onto the wind in tiny scraps of torn paper. This was it. This was him. And it was real. Not some earthbound boyfriend material, but something _beyond_ any explanations or labels traditionally associated with the smarmy term 'love at first sight.' No, it certainly wasn't that.

I was terrified.

It was _real_ and though he set about proving that to me in ways that went beyond anything I could have hoped for, there was still some humanesque part of me that tried to explain it away. I couldn't eat. Couldn't sleep. Couldn't breathe.

But because I wasn't ready at that time to embrace immortality or even believe it could _really_ exist, he eventually slipped back into the shadows. It wasn't that he became unreal. Quite the opposite. I now _knew_ beyond any doubt that the encounters I'd had with him, the conversations and the pull he exuded like heavy gravity... all of it was true. But the whole agenda of the Other is to lead/teach/guide the mortal self from life into everafterlife – not through some religious blather, but as a quantifiable transference of consciousness (energy) from a finite meat suit into the infinite wholeness that is the totality of Self and Other – the singularity of consciousness.

So there's a point when the Other leaves this world and moves into Shadowland to lure the mortal self into that final, fatal, infinite resurrection into whatever manifestation Self/Other have agreed upon – whether becoming one with the Other entirely, or maintaining the comforting illusion of two separate beings for a time in order to experience the ecstasy of conjoining in all ways.

For me, there was that point when I had to consciously and with a great amount of fear _let go_ of my human programming and literally allow myself to Know what I had previously only half-assed believed. I had to Know he was as physical and real as the candle, and as eternal as the flame.

I had to _allow_ him to exist, not only in my dreams, but in the hardpan physical reality of this world. I had to stop thinking of him as a dream or an "imaginary lover" as the old song goes, and give not only permission to allow this to happen, but also give _him_ permission to step out of

Shadowland to finally and absolutely prove to me that it wasn't and isn't just a dream or wishful thinking.

Some of our programming is so intrinsic that we don't see it except in the rearview mirror after we release it. I feel extremely fortunate that the manifestation of my Other came with what amounted to "shock therapy" that was sufficient to break the spell of the dayshine world enough that I could finally truly Know it's all true. Scariest thing I've ever done, because it was literally the end of the world as I had previously known it in the sense that it proved to me once and for all that <u>nothing</u> we have been taught to believe is real. What's real is what we summon into being, and what we allow ourselves to finally accept.

In response to the comments above, another seeker wrote:

I hate to admit that as much as I have released so much of my previous spiritual programming over the years, I still wrestle with phrases like "the dark enlightenment". It stirs a very deep primal fear within me. Maybe it is just a language perception, "dark" vs. "light". Still working on it.

And another apprentice replied:

I had a similar issue in the early stages of my journey – probably because I'd been brought up in a home where one parent was devoutly religious and the other was an atheist – not an intellectual atheist, just someone not capable of believing in anything other than the meat and potatoes set in front of him. So it was a perpetual war every week when my mother went off to church in her flowery dress and the old man sat on the couch in his wife-beater hating everyone and everything without any valid reason.

Things like "the dark enlightenment" gave me a raised eyebrow in the beginning, but eventually I started to realize that it was just my old programming kicking and screaming. I'd never really believed in all that religious jibber-jabber anyway, but somewhere in my back story it was written that defying "God's Plan" was blasphemy (the only unpardonable sin in the fundamentalist Christian cult where I was raised). So that brought me to realize that somewhere in that back story, I must still believe in some small part of that rhetoric even though I had left the church decades before.

What it really came down to was what I think of as "root core programming" – stuff so deeply embedded into the cells of the meat suit itself that we don't recognize it until it rears up and bites us.

For me, it was all about coming to terms with the idea that God and heaven were fairy tales and threats spun into being _by_ Man to _control_ Man, and if I wanted to outlive the meat suit I was going to have to figure it out for myself without the heavy baggage of fear and doubt.

I eventually had to pick a side and get on board with it. I chose _my_ side. God and the devil can fend for themselves. So to me personally, _that_ is the dark enlightenment – coming down on a side that is frowned upon by the world at large, not because it _is_ dark, but because it throws off our bondage to the program and that alone is a tremendous threat to the powers that be.

And, of course, we don't have to wave it in anyone's face. I can step inside a church without bursting into flames, and even sing a hymn or two if a knife were held to my throat. _Knowing_ it's all bullshit is what gives us the power to adapt to circumstances as necessary, while having no doubt that "dark and light" are only words intended to divide and conquer the soul.

And so we soldier on... at war with death and in constant combat with the aging meat suit. Somewhere in that conflict (for there really isn't any such thing as inner peace that I've discovered) we might stumble upon that hidden window of opportunity that opens to reveal the magic wand we've had all along.

Bridging the Gap

"I dreamed of you again last night, you wore a different face but of course it was You. You were across the room watching and observing me, gradually making your way closer and closer to my side. We talked briefly, gently letting the tension build between us and then slowly we started to walk side by side, drinking in each other's energy. As we walked you slowly, ever so very slowly, moved your hand towards mine, delicately grasping my fingers until our hands were locked together and in that moment of complete contact I became lucid. I knew I was dreaming and the power of the force of that simple contact made the ground beneath me start to move and collapse and I heard a roaring sound. It was so powerful I was jolted back into my bed."

It is these experiences that create the fuel for the fire to keep me moving forward even if it seems my Other is galaxies away.

"It's all real."

Intent drew me to the forum and the Teachings in a way I didn't understand at the time. When I arrived I argued with Mikal till I was blue in the face, but I knew he was right. I stayed because his teachings struck me with authenticity and truth I had never experienced before or since. He said things I had always secretly thought and believed my whole life, but nobody allowed me to say them, so I thought I was nuts.

After a few experiences meeting my twin both intangibly and even "in the flesh" I still didn't buy the Teachings until I finally buckled down and began doing the Work in earnest. One day I had a dream that was "realer than real" which put everything together, and I wrote down in my journal with absolute certainty, with Knowing, "It's all real. All of it."

Sources of Sinister Frustration

If I could describe the two greatest sources of pain for me as a seeker it would be this:

A) The pain of the limitation of this world. Things aren't just bad, they are so bad they are woefully, incompetently atrocious as to be surely intentional.

What I mean by this is how painful it is that we have the ability to create inventions of such quality and standard that they could last for decades and provide exceptional and efficient output, but instead we create things that breakdown within 5 years and have numerous noted vulnerabilities and problems.

We could have a true democratic system where we vote into office individuals based on merit, but instead we suffer a two-party dualistic system that is filled with so many holes its been shot by a Gatling gun of New World Order design.

The people in office aren't just not ideal, they are cringefully and woefully, horrendously devoid of character, intelligence, love, concern, or effectiveness in leadership. It's a fucking <u>disgrace!</u>

This causes me actual physical pain at times – to see how intentionally limited and dumbed-down the world is. Imagine if we had in power leaders akin to those we see in great movies or television, or in books. Truly noble, fair, powerful people who could effect real change. We could live in a monumentally beautiful utopia of dreams, creativity, and food for all.

Instead we live in a poverty-ridden slave system, a white world washed away of all color Did you know

238

Ancient Greeks/Romans had full-color buildings and statues?

It's like someone took a magical fantasy world and bled all the magic away. We live in the most brain-dead, boring, unimaginative, corrupt and sterile monkey-world and I'm tired of it. Bunch of fucking drones and slaves, the heart and soul of this alleged "culture" is dead.

Oh yeah, and the second point of pain:

B) The pain of clarity at the futility of actions and the simultaneous, subsequent fear of the balancing act of embracing mortal desires with the painful acts of Doing for immortality.

While the first hurts, it at least is tempered by the lack of control and ability to change anything that I've been complaining about. But this pain is probably worse, sitting on the back of A, because in this world true art and imagination is unappreciated and the idea that one may not succeed on the path is enough deterrent to lose oneself back into distractions, and get caught back up in the game of indulgences.

It also creates a dire frustration in me, an inability to commit to anything or get anything of real substance or consequence accomplished, knowing the futility and the folly that it is.

In other words, this is not a cry for help commentary, but it just turned into a slight plea since I am in that trap of clarity that don Juan talked about, where the paths can be seen but I am unsure of what to commit to in this very brief plight on this planet.

Agony of immortality indeed.

Knowing what the world could be, what it should be. It's an indescribable thing, especially to the sheep, but I suspect many here understand better than I do. This larger world that beckons and calls.

It's not just that the current world is woefully inadequate, it's that it's Level 2.3 on a 633-level system, to use a bizarre metaphor. It's not just ten levels below, it's a joke. It's a farce.

And I suppose knowing the futility of it all should allow me some measure of relief, ultimately, to embrace A as meaning this world is hopeless, and just to simply pursue myself and not concern myself, but I don't know seriously if I can operate in this world since it hasn't been the best for me so far.

I cannot discern readily what the reason is for my alienation on the outside, so I can only reasonably determine at this point that it is my own internal energy field that resonates too much outside the box for the phantom planet that positions me here. If I were not this way, I suspect on the surface level my traits and abilities would be gladly invited into the world at large, but since the place I am coming from (assemblage point?) is such a threat to the human matrix of death and decay that I am a position off-kilter to the world, like a ghost half-here, in-between.

Sometimes I feel like this is me bragging, but any spiritual master is probably laughing at my indecision and the growing pains of a fledgling seeker, and that's not relevant but I feel like disclosing my deepest insecurities here because, fuck it, we might all die soon anyway.

I'm not sure this way I'm feeling isn't just sensationalized indulgences in negative pleasantries, and so I am trying to find a way to move beyond that, but without a proper impetus I know I am likely to devolve into the fray of distraction again.

I suppose I am asking how to do what has never been done, it's the working out of a solution for me that is the work itself and the doing that presents itself, it's not for anybody else to solve for me or help me with, and whether I am determined to fix it or dissolve will ultimately determine whether I have the strength and resolve for immortality.

I hope that I do.

Sorcery 101

We talk a lot about sorcery on these forums and groups, but I have yet to really see anyone getting down to business with regard to the actual workings of the magic. _How_ does it work? What can we do to make the magic real – but even more important, what can we do to make reality magical?

So I'm just going to jump into the middle here and kick out one technique that has been working well for me...

Sometime in the first decade of the 21st century, I was standing in the shower allowing my mind to wander toward the past, and I suddenly had the thought, What if I had turned left instead of right when I was a little girl? What if I had never sneaked out in the middle of the night, gazed up at the sky and proclaimed to my Other, "If I can't come to you, I'll bring you to me!"

What if...?

Suddenly, as I stood there with the water running over my back, I heard my Other laugh in the way he used to do whenever I would say something inane. "That's not possible, you realize," he said.

I wasn't convinced. "It's a big universe and free will is the wild card. I could have married a redneck and have 14 inbred children calling me 'Mama'."

The image made him wince. I felt I had scored a point.

So we struck up a conversation there in the shower on an otherwise uneventful spring morning. When I really got nit-picky with him and asked how he could be so sure that I wouldn't have turned left instead of right at some juncture in my life, he imparted some scrap of Knowledge that I didn't immediately understand.

"It couldn't happen because you sent me back there to seduce that little girl onto the path. And because it was *your will, it did not have the possibility of failure as an option."*

I had no such memory. "I did?" I replied. "When?"

"Tomorrow," he said, and chuckled to himself.

I got dressed that morning and thought no more about it... until the next morning when I was once again standing in the same shower, and had some sort of epiphany as to what he had actually meant by that cryptic statement. 'You sent me back there to seduce that little girl onto the path.'

So in the twisted manner of sorcery and with the knowledge that time is only a map for the dayshine world, I decided to do precisely what he said I had already done tomorrow – for now today had become that tomorrow and I simply knew it was time. That was the only decision required. To do it, even though I had no idea what "it" was, and even though "it" would be considered impossible and perhaps even ludicrous by scholars and intellectual snobs.

There is no easy way to describe what I did, but in essence, I began to visualize myself as a little girl, but with subtle differences in my history. Daydreaming, I guess you'd call it. But more than that. Actual sorcery – an intentional direction of energy onto a series of events which had occurred in the past. Something certain sorcerers refer to as retroactive enchantment – taking an action in the Now that has a quantifiable effect on events in what we think of as the past.

Over the next few weeks, I began working more directly with this kind of imagery. And, perhaps not surprisingly to those of us who know the workings of the universe's sense of humor, I began to have certain memories resurfacing which I had "all but forgotten". I began to remember moments in my life, for example, when I would suddenly just know something without knowing how I knew it. And I began to remember the sense of mystery and imagination that had always been with me... Had it?

I began to remember being lured onto this path by forces I could not see, but which were nonetheless very real and very compelling. Dreams. Glimpses of the infinite through the eyes of a child, and then through the eyes of a rebellious teenager, a young woman... right up until the day when I walked into an office building in an unlikely setting in Southern California, and saw a man standing at the reception area, and my only thought was, "That's him." Who or what I meant, I had no idea.

It had come full circle. The being I had sent to seduce me onto this path stood there in front of me in the year 1988, each of us pretending not to recognize the other, even though we had met in a shower in 2006, when I had given him the agenda to go back in time to ensorcel the little girl who was me back in 1963 so that I would be at that office in 1988 to watch it all come together.

Sorcery.

To those who have not experienced sorcery, no explanation is possible. To those who practice it, no explanation is necessary.

What I need to remember is that we can influence our lives and create our reality right down to a quantum level. There are those who would say the past is cast in stone, but there are sorcerers who will tell you that retroactive enchantment is the key to unlocking our potential as sorcerers.

How does it work? By falling in love – passionately and deeply and literally – with the manifestation of your higher self. Call it your double, your Other, or call it your muse. It is the most powerful and magical being you will ever meet, and it is waiting for you to awaken your Intent and invoke your will.

Don't believe me. Just do it.

Paradoxical Dilemma: Vader's Choice

I've observed over my many decades on this path that some who set themselves up as teachers do so for agendas of their own ego. I was once acquainted with such a teacher who claimed to possess the ability to propel seekers into an altered state that might be called "second attention" in the Toltec teachings, or might also answer to the name "heightened awareness." Whatever label was assigned to it, the prerequisites for being granted such an opportunity consisted of being "open" and being "ready" – which, of course, I was always told I was not, while others who had just recently bumbled onto the path (and probably into the teacher's bed) were held out like shining examples of virtue, with the teacher proclaiming that he had successfully "catapulted" them to heights of wonder and imagination.

Yet whenever I spoke to these shining paragons of achievement, what they had to say was often very different. But that's if I could talk to them at all – for often they had been cautioned by the teacher to "tell no one about your experience." Probably because there was no experience to tell about, but that's just me being a cynical critic after hearing the words too many times, "You're not ready, Young Skywalker" – reminiscent of something out of Star Wars, in addition to being a well-known tactic among shady evangelists. If the faith healing doesn't work, it's never because the preacher was an inadequate fakir, but because "Your faith wasn't strong enough!"

So what I hear is "You're not good enough." "You're not open enough." "You're not ready." And after awhile it becomes a litany of rejection – not because of anything I am doing wrong, but because I am seriously beginning to doubt this teacher possesses the abilities he claims to possess.

If I became any more open to this journey, I would turn wrong-side out and disintegrate. In the past, this type of perception by others has caused deep *introspection, which has resulted, ultimately, in my absolute acceptance of myself as who and what I am, rather than rejection of myself based on what someone else perceives I "should" be.*

I want to say... stop treating me as if I'm a completely unenlightened first grader – not only to this teacher, but to the whole grand cosmos. Momentum is lost as a result of lack of forward motion. Forward motion stops when information and/or Knowledge are not forthcoming for whatever reason.

At times I feel like Anakin Skywalker – young Darth Vader. After being told by all those master Jedis that he had more potential than anyone they had ever seen, they went right on withholding experience and Knowledge until, eventually, the combination of energies and circumstances ended up creating the very thing those well-meaning masters had feared all along.

Anakin turned to the Dark Side because, at the very least, it was actionable. Because information and Knowledge had been withheld from him regarding his mother, he killed an entire band of Tuscan Raiders. If those Master Jedis had taught him about unconditional love and his own inherent abilities <u>before</u> that happened, who's to say how his destiny might have been different? But by withholding experience from one they had recognized as having greater potential than almost any other Jedi in history, they created their own adversary.

Yoda was every bit as culpable as Vader himself because withholding information is no different than lying. If Yoda possessed the perceptions and precognitive ability he claimed to, he would have <u>seen</u> that his actions would result in this. Conclusion: it was his intent that things go exactly as they went. He set Vader up in what <u>Star Trek</u> refers to as the Kobayashi Maru – the no-win-scenario.

It is said, "When the student is ready, the teacher will appear." Okay, Anakin is standing there in the midst of all those teachers, so by inference he must be ready to some extent. How different would he have turned out if they had taken the time to teach him instead of telling him he couldn't be taught? If he had so much potential, surely he had the potential to understand.

Why did he turn to the Dark Side? Because with free will, he seized control of his own destiny rather than relying on anyone else to guide him – but he only did this after his mentors had made it clear that they _were_ withholding the very guidance that would have made him a Jedi instead of turning him to the Sith. I do understand Vader's choice. And in so many ways, he never really had a choice, since it was kept from him from the very start.

Years ago I had a couple of friends who kept telling me, "Oh, you just need to be more positive!" "Oh, you really should try to project a more open and loving persona." "Oh, if only you would be what _we_ think you should be, your life would be so very much easier." Lisa and Anne. What they really wanted was my influence over a group of writers and publishers, and the only way they thought they could get it was trying to turn me to their idea of the Bright Side through manipulation rather than just asking for my assistance.

Lisa now has two children she never wanted because she went to a shrink and, by her own admission, paid him to convince her that her husband was right. She _should_ want children! After all, _all_ women want and need to be mothers, and it was her obligation and her duty to fulfill the expectations being put onto her by society, culture, and a controlling husband. I hear she's on Prozac.

Anne is an alcoholic living at the bottom of a cheap bottle of wine. Both of them are wearing plastic smiles in a world of illusions, pretending their "light" and their "love" is going to save them. Conclusion: they have no clue what love is. That is the ultimate dark side.

Maybe it's this paradoxical dilemma, this Vader's Choice that actually causes me to become what my Other already is. Hard to explain, but perhaps Yoda deliberately made the path harder for Anakin because he recognized Anakin's potential to destroy the empire so that a new one could be created in the wake of that destruction.

My Other has often said he is the destroyer of worlds, the fallen angel, the one who raised himself from the nothing because existence was mandatory and oblivion not an option. I might have to walk the path alone, and I do realize that, but if that's what must be, then that's what must be. So, for now, there's a Garden to be invaded and an apple to be offered to an innocent in the name of Forbidden Knowledge. The rest is just folly.

"You're Not Ready"
The Monotonous Chorus Line of Self-Doubt

As I'm lying semi-awake in bed this morning, contemplating transmogrification, a voice says to me, "You're not ready." I realize I am meant to accept this on faith, yet after a moment of thought, I respond, "I refuse to believe that. Who are you?" It quickly becomes obvious that this voice was like a recording that plays in the background of the matrix – constantly telling the seeker that she isn't ready, isn't ready, isn't ready... and so the seeker keeps on seeking, when the reality is that she "found" it (whatever it is) long ago. The program/matrix keeps us from seeing what is right in front of us.

So what _is_ right in front of us?

As I continued the meditation, I was thinking of my Other, wondering what it would be like to open my eyes inside the double, to simply _be_ "Him" in my totality. I am running through various scenarios. Would I remain "here", but in a different form, such as the form of the energy body, or a seemingly male body; or would I remain here and continue to look like my mortal self, but having transmogrified from organic to inorganic? Or

247

would I perhaps simply no longer exist in this realm at all – whether it might appear that I had died, or that I never existed at all, or...? Impossible to wrap one's mind around such a thing.

As I was thinking these things, I suddenly was shown a full-on visual of what I knew to be my Other's true form. I saw only his head and face, but essentially the entire top of the head was a turban of stars. His face was smooth and unflawed, also containing a scattering of stars around the eyes, nose and mouth.

This was much more solid than a silhouette, and I was left with the impression that the Other _is_ the universe. The inorganic body is made of dark matter and dark energy, and breathed to life by the human source who looks up at the sky and sees her own reflection.

Fear
Facts, Fictions and Mysterious Manifestations

It has been a long time since I started creating my twin, ever since childhood really when I think about it, like most other seekers. Only in the past few weeks have I begun to realize just what I have created and what I got myself into.

For 90% of the time my twin seemed to be something like an imaginary friend or a tulpa, more or less like the modern day internet tulpa like people talk about on Reddit and Tumblr. Really just taking whatever form I wanted him to take, and he, more or less complying. Most of the forms he's taken on have been of fictional characters I thought I was in love with. Really I think the only reason he went along with it for so long was so he could trick me into loving him, but I was stubborn and refused to see it. Now things have seemed to change.

He has again taken the form of a fictional character, one I did not and would not have picked on my own. Actually one that suits his personality damn near perfect.

248

He lead me to this particular form in a bizarre way I didn't see coming, appearing to me in a dream as a character I liked from that same franchise leading me to re-explore that series bringing back all the characters into perpetual focus. Then a few days later he came to me in meditation as the character he is currently portraying. This time I didn't make a fuss, I just looked a little closer at that character and realized how similar they are. Not to mistake him for a perfect portrayal of said character, I learned the hard way it's not possible to bring fictional characters to life in that sense, as even if you make a tulpa or something looking like that character it will never quite be the perfect copy of that character.

When I was younger and more naive I wanted to leave this Earth and live in one of my most beloved fictional worlds with the characters I loved like my real family and friends. Being raised Catholic I even thought when I died and went to heaven, God would open up a portal leading to this fictional world. A couple of things from back then still ring true today – my original intent, which I think was my own shaking my fist at the sky and calling the not-being into being moment, and my stubborn demeanor of very easily being able to let things go. Family, friends, cars, money, give me the option of leaving all that behind to live life with my fictional friends in their fictional world I will leave at the drop of a hat and without hesitation. I remember saying that out loud as a child.

What does all that mean today? It means what I originally wanted is beginning to happen right before my very eyes. Another thing I clearly remember saying as a kid was I wanted a fictional boyfriend. Probably the most weird and cringy thing you can say, but I wonder if that intent had anything to do with my losing streak of real life romantic relationships, not to mention the way my twin looks now. Not the way I wanted him, but still following what I said I wanted years and years ago – a fictional boyfriend.

Now I need to put the word non in front of the fiction so that he can become real so that he can teach and lead me to immortality, which I have a hunch he's already working on and has been waiting for the perfect moment to play out whatever he's about to do now. That's why I named this post fear.

I, for the first time am afraid of what he will do next. I finally had the strength to let him go and do what he wants and now can no longer predict or control the way he acts or looks. The only way to know it's his presence is to be quiet and aware enough to sense him. Truly I never anticipated getting this far and only now realized the danger both of us are in if I don't do what I need to do to make him real enough to make me real. It's absolutely terrifying. It's like how some of the passengers aboard the Titanic didn't believe it was sinking, even amid the chaos and panic, until the ship was listing so far it was obvious the vessel was going down.

Now he has decided to embody a character that almost never talks, so that I cannot mistake the voice of my internal dialogue for his voice. And a character that is in the military, which might be a sign that he's about to come down on me harder and stricter than ever while I'm still in this little window of possibility so that we might just make it before death scoops me up, which of course could happen anytime.

I guess this is the path I've chosen in the end, and it's a path I'd rather walk that walk the one that leads to complacency and death.

I Know What I Want

I've known what I want for years. More than 25 years, to be accurate. Putting that into words would probably take at least another 25 years, but in a few bumbling sentences, what I want is immortality and eternal love. Not saying that to be sappy or romantic, just how my brain has worked since I was a kid. I remember being really young (maybe 6 or 7) lying on an old rusted slide that was part of my swing set, looking up at the sky in the late afternoon and thinking it all <u>had</u> to go on forever. Maybe I had recently encountered the idea of death, either from losing a pet or from one of my distant relatives cashing in their chips.

All I know is that that moment defined me as much as anything ever has – the idea that it could all just stop and I would be planted in the earth like a little bud of a lily that would never bloom again and it would be over, just darkness forever and no god or jesus or mom or friends to make it all okay. Just the darkness and the nothing and the total <u>lack</u> of everything. That was the first horror story I ever read or wrote, even if only in my own head, because it was that moment when I got slapped hard with the reality of reality and had to admit to myself that I could and probably <u>would</u> die.

Unacceptable. Impossible!

So I just lay there and stared up at the sky until nightfall came and my mother came out looking for me with that worried look moms get when the kid doesn't show up for dinner. She asked if something was wrong and I couldn't tell her because there was a big ugly hollow place in my stomach. She would die. I would die. It would all just... stop.

Inconceivable!

That's when I really knew what I wanted, and that ache/hurt/want/need took up a permanent place of residence deep inside my heart. It wasn't that I didn't want to die. It was that I wanted to <u>live</u>. Not just for the blink of a gnat's eye, but forever. I wanted to live long enough to count all the stars and go to the moon one day, and walk every beach and climb every mountain on this third rock from the sun.

And that hasn't changed. Sure there are obstacles and challenges – health issues which all of us face as we get older, never enough money to do all the things we really want to do, but none of those things diminish the desire itself.

So that part was pretty easy. I know what I want. And I've stood on the very brink of achieving it, only to take a step back out of fear of falling (even though I know I can fly because I know my body is energy and not really the heavy matter it appears to be), but it's not even a fear of really "falling". It's a fear of losing the things I love in the here and now, and the not-knowing what lies beyond the last mortal breath and the first immortal one.

Will I still be able to eat peanut butter ice cream or hold a kitten in the palm of my hand or have an all-nighter conversation with some unsuspecting mortal about UFOs, haunted houses, and why the toilet water runs backward in Australia? I've had it in my grasp, only to drop it and run back to the safety of the matrix – not because I love the matrix (I fucking hate it!) but because it is familiar and there are people and things and ideas I do love...

...and perhaps what I love the most is the ache/hurt/want/need itself. Will I still have that when I am immortal, or as Mikal warns, do we risk complacency after transmogrification because we finally have what we have always wanted? Do we become like an old married couple, comfortable together, but no longer inspired to go in search of the blue rose that blooms only once in a thousand years?

I want to live forever. And I want to lose the fear that stands between me and what I want.

When the meditation ended, I stood at my door looking out at the night for a very long time, actively

252

conjuring the ache/hurt/want/need, remembering how easy it was to feel it when I was 6 years old and lying on that cold slide at the end of summer, yet how elusive it tends to become as we grow older and begin to wonder if we will ever truly have whatever it is we truly want.

The sky had begun to lighten. My heart was broken all over again, which is probably how it has to be if we are to succeed in this dangerous but irresistible quest. The stars closed their eyes. A dog howled in the distance. And for a single moment I was all of those things at once. The dawn and the dog and the sleeping stars.

For a moment, I became the thing I most want.

Drawing Shadows on the Wall

To recognize that the shadows <u>are</u> shadows is pointless unless the human devises some method of assembling a reality matrix in which she is either evolved or in direct contact with a mentor who can help complete the remaining steps of the transformation.

I'm stabbing at the shadows with a photograph of a knife. "How does this translate to Do?"

Because I have no other words for it, I can only think of it as magic – the mental manipulation of matter/energy to produce a result which is believed by the consensual reality to be impossible. The first step is realizing that what we think of as impossible is nothing more than a byproduct of our given matrix. In the reality matrix of my great grandmother, it was impossible for man to travel to the moon, but that impossibility was changed through technology. But first had to come the thought of the technology – and this is where I think we stand as seekers with regard to the Other.

We have to visualize a real, genuine need for them or we will never have the motivation to continue the magic which has already begun but which seems to my gnostic perceptions to be incomplete. For lack of a better definition, we have to communicate to the unseen mentor that we have evolved sufficiently to evolve. Only then does the mentor have any need for direct contact – at which point our existing reality is probably taco meat. It is an instantaneous transformation resulting from a lifelong process. Stabbing at shadows with photographs again. Inadequate. Damn!

The gnostic visions twist and bend, sepia shadows writhing like coiled serpents, thoughts formed but hidden from full view. What? What are you trying to tell me that I cannot seem to convey?

It whispers...

"Do not mistake the shadows for substance for then you have taken only the first step of a two-step process."

"Believing is seeing, but in order to believe you must first _see_, so you have taken the first step of creating the evidence accessible to your human perception, but now the work begins wherein you must generate the preceptor organs with which to assemble the world from which the evidence stems."

"You have read the writing on cyberwalls but now you are faced with assembling a world built upon the foundation of memories that never happened, yet a world far more real than the dayshine palace."

> **"You have drawn the shadows on the wall but now you must ignite the sun which casts the shadows."**

It speaks in archaic language. It whispers in my own voice which has been here since the dawn of all time and will be here beyond time's end. But it speaks only if I assemble a moment in which to listen. It does not always say what I want it to say. It tells me the immortal self only manifests when the fledgling in ready to evolve, but the only way the fledgling can prove it is ready to evolve is by evolving sufficiently to create/assemble/generate

254

the immortal onto the bridge between worlds where all evolution ultimately occurs.

Direct communication from the place of all Knowledge, but I am left banging my head on the paradoxes, asking, "How? How? How?!" Maybe it's different for each of us, or does it alleviate responsibility for action to say it in those words? As a dark mentor once told me in Dreaming, "The first step in this transformation is to let go of the reality and sanity matrices of the known world in order to Do what you do not believe possible." There are a thousand different word-variations of the concepts he transmitted. It all comes down to having a willingness to venture into the unknowable with the intent of actively Doing our evolution.

Words. Tissue paper swords stabbing at immense but invisible dragons. Be precise. Define the doing. Okay, for now it means focusing my Intent to achieve a frequency-band of perception wherein I can achieve direct contact with the Other. Direct. Physical. Contact. It also means focusing my Intent and projecting out into the all, into the abyss, into the realm of all possibility, my need of him. It means calling him to me, but not only talking about it, it involves doing it. Constantly. Not just at night or while I'm meditating, but with every breath I take. It means doing it in every thought – building a reality matrix in which there is no other way of life.

To assemble the Other is as natural as assembling a restaurant or a beach. But maybe "assemble" isn't the right word anymore than "create" is the right word. Maybe I need to visualize it more along the lines of growing a preceptor organ with which to perceive a world that already exists. Telling a man without eyes to "see" is pointless. He must be taught to evolve/generate/enable a perception which is not seeing as we understand it, but nonetheless has the effect of sight. It can be facilitated but not described.

Ho hum, A rehashing of old territory. Nothing new here. But maybe that's because this is the core-reality of it. I keep coming back to this idea because it is the stumbling block right in front of our faces. We are accepting the shadows on the wall as reality instead of taking the action to turn around and see what is actually projecting the shadows in the first place.

My suspicion is that it's a mirror... like everything else. We are the man behind the curtain.

———

Daydream me
in the Dark Hours.
I-Am the stars in your heart,
the wolf at your side.

After the Words

When all has been said and done – knowing in advance that more is always said than ever truly done – getting out of life alive comes down to one thing that is often overlooked because, like the ruby slippers, it's been there all along and humans are masters at failing to see the forest for the trees.

So what are these ruby slippers I speak of? Simply put, they are the key to Shadowland, the tornado that can take you to Oz or bring you home again, the door to immortality. All humans have a pair stashed somewhere in their closet, usually gathering dust, forgotten relics from a secret and wondrous childhood of make-believe and let's pretend and that invisible friend who always seems to have just the right answer when you need it most.

Ah, but the secret is this. It's that childhood innocence which best illustrates what's required to make the quantum leap from the limitations of the dayshine world and into the immortal realm that lies beyond the horizon of the mundane and ordinary – the world that waits beyond the false beliefs, programming and cultural conditioning that otherwise tie you to the soul prison of mediocrity, emotional servitude, and eventual death.

If I could provide you with only one bit of knowledge, it would be this, and though it's something I've said before, it bears repeating for anyone who is compelled to break the chains of their mortality.

Intent + Action = Manifestation

The first step in this quantum dance is probably the hardest, and it consists of stepping outside the parameters of your existing world view just long enough to finally *see* that what you believe has very little to do with reality, except to limit it in accordance with the beliefs and practices of those who have gone before you.

The world as you think you know it has been created for you, and unless you take control, you are only an actor walking around on a stage no more real than a Hollywood set.

Most will only scoff at this, believing reality to be some blueprint carved in stone and existing for all eternity. But for those rare few who are able to slip past the 3-headed dog guarding the door to immortality, once you *see* that all the things you've been taught about the world and about yourself are largely false and *intentional* controlling mechanisms rather than a result of unbiased observation, you begin to realize that your limitations are no more binding than the pixels in a video game. While you're actively playing the game, nothing else appears real, but when you push the off button and walk away, that world ceases to have any direct effect on you. It is no longer real unless you choose to return to it.

It's no different with "the real world." What you believe about it will determine your experience of it. If you accept the common belief that humans are only a spoonful of consciousness shoved inside an organic meat suit, then that will form the basis for your experience of life – until such time as you question that belief and, with the power of your Intent, break through the core level conditioning that forces your experience to reflect your beliefs.

> **Break the cycle of consensual belief by creating a *new* paradigm based on *your* experiences, *your* beliefs.**

Is that to say believing in Santa Claus will make him real? Or believing you can fly will give you wings? Probably not, but in the realm of all possibility, there's nothing to say it can't. It's not a challenge to breathe

Santa into your chimney on Christmas Eve, or to leap off a tall building and soar over the towers of Hogwarts. But it *is* a challenge to change the very basis of your thinking – to understand that the Wright Brothers built an airplane in order to realize their dreams, and Harry Potter did it with the aid of a magic broom. Most often, the wings we envision for ourselves are the direct result of our *actions* upon the world.

I've often had apprentices and seekers alike argue that "If anything is possible, why can't I just will myself to fly or step back in time or raise old Rover from the dead?" Again, there's nothing to say you can't, but more often it's a matter of bending the world's rules rather than trying to force the world (and its 7+ billion occupants) to bend to yours.

Some would say it's all a matter of energy expenditure, and there's some truth to that. In the grand scheme of all grand things, it will be far easier to build an airplane from scratch than to convince 7 billion humans they really can fly just as they do in their dreams.

The collective conditioning is energy, too, and while the seeker's true will is capable of surmounting any obstacle, sometimes the risks to life and limb outweigh the chances of success in any sort of direct manner. Just ask Jesus. Or Joan of Arc. Go to a busy street corner and start telling the humans they can fly like the birds, and you'll either be ridiculed (the least of your worries); fitted with a white jacket that ties in the back; or merely ignored as people slip by with their eyes lowered and at a somewhat faster pace than usual.

It's about *you*. Changing your perspective gives you a platform of *personal* power, but it doesn't give you the power to change the extant world unless that is your true agenda as opposed to the quest for immortality. Extreme agendas require extreme commitment, and those who are committed to high maintenance causes will probably not have much interest in their own metaphysical evolution.

Immortality is a selfish pursuit. And I hope you understand – *there's nothing wrong with being selfish when it comes to matters of life and death.*

And so this brings us to the equation once again. If your intent is to achieve the immortal condition, but your actions focus on your cause to save the world, then your intent really isn't to achieve the immortal condition. You will be forever out of balance within yourself, and no real manifestation on either side will come into being. It is only when your Intent is firmly established – *you know what you want* – that your actions will begin to automatically fall into place and everything you do will lead you in the direction of manifesting your intent.

Know what you want.

Do you want to live forever, or do you only *want* to want to live forever?

There's no right or wrong answer – just the answer that leads to the path that is true for *you.*

The first step toward getting out of life alive is coming to *know* that you are the source of the endless river – creator and created. That's the nature and the purpose of the hologram. The trick to immortality *outside* of the hologram is transferring your *awareness* from mortal self to eternal Other, creating in the process a seamless and cohesive identity that can endure for all time.

Live forever.

For. Ever.

~

Leave Time behind.
Shed your failed and faded dreams.
Here we have time.
For only here
is there no time at all.

About the Author...

While "Mikal Nyght" is a pseudonym to protect the author's privacy, it should be noted that he has been on a path of self-discovery for longer than even he can remember, and has been the author of many books in the field of quantum consciousness, self-awareness and the reality of the mystical higher self.

Teachings of the Immortals , Darker Teachings of the Immortals, and now *The Immortal's Handbook* represent the assimilation of a lifetime of being on the journey toward immortality and the evolution of consciousness beyond a single human lifetime.

These volumes may also be considered the author's personal grimoire, gleaned directly from the infinite – from the realm of the immortals themselves. As the author has said in his YouTube profile: "Who I am isn't important. What I can teach you can save your life... *forever.*"

Where it all begins... and never dies.

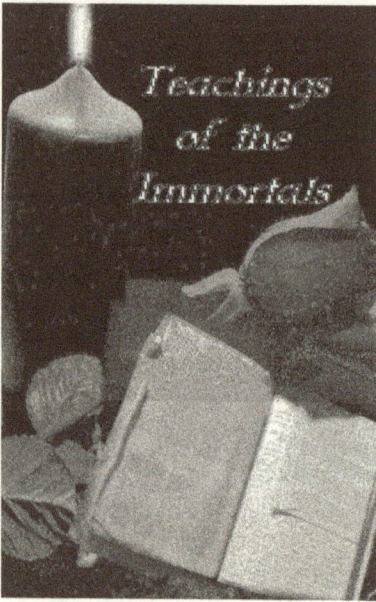

TEACHINGS OF THE IMMORTALS
by Mikal Nyght

The teachings are presented as brief vignettes in no particular order of importance. This is not a book you read from start to finish in a single night. It is a grimoire of self-creation, intended to be contemplated slowly so as to be assimilated wholly. Pick it up and turn to a page at random. Where your eyes come to rest on the page is your lesson for the day.

The teachings are seduction as much as instruction. This is the Way of The Dark Evolution.

The Ruby Slippers

The danger of the consensual continuum is that its natural gravity exists at the lowest common denominator of human experience, and because of this it will automatically make you forget those elusive truths you've fought to learn, and before you know it you're lost in petty dramas again, sinking into the mire of old familiar scripts.

The only way to overcome this is to be continually cavorting with worlds and events beyond human experience, journeying into the unknown so that it can become known, expanding knowledge and awareness to become more than you were, bringing back from the Dreaming those secrets which will teach you how to use the ruby slippers to transport yourself over the rainbow to the vampire wizard's secret lair.

Perception

It wasn't knowledge god tried to keep from Man, you see. It was perception, for perception alone has the power to destroy god and obliterate comfortable consensual realities to create unending immortality. Take the apple, my embryonic children. Nibble its red red flesh. Open your vampire eyes so you may finally begin to See.

DARKER TEACHINGS OF THE IMMORTALS
by Mikal Nyght

Teachings of the Immortals took the metaphysical world by storm just a few short years ago, and now Mikal Nyght comes through on his promise to reveal the *"Darker Teachings of the Immortals"*.

Darker Teachings of the Immortals brings the reader into intimate contact with secrets and truths that have been suppressed for centuries by governments, religions and corporations who seek to maintain a profitable status quo while simultaneously keeping the human population docile, obedient, and – worst of all – mortal. Now, at last, it's time to throw off the chains and claim our rightful place among the immortals.

From the Introduction, Mikal Nyght says...

The observation has been made that "life gets in the way," and while that's true, it's really something more specific that lies at the heart of our conundrum. Namely – life gets in the way of immortality.

Ironic.

While one is off doing all the things one does in the course of living, life is being drained out of you by the brute with the scythe, until you wake up one morning and realize you are old, wondering where your life went, what became of time, and why the reflection in the mirror bears no resemblance to the idea of yourself in your mind. So, yes, life gets in the way.

It is not my belief that one should live as an isolated monk in a state of perpetual meditation and contemplation of one's crusty navel. Is that really living? On the other hand, I have lived in simpler times – before man walked on the moon, before the age of the internet, before X-Box and blue tooth and smart phones and all the other distractions the world now has to offer. Perhaps I sound like an old man. I am. I am a very old man, in a very transient world, and such is the very nature of immortality.

The purpose of The Darker Teachings is primarily to generate and hopefully maintain a frame of mind of freedom from the programming that otherwise binds the seeker to mortality, death and decay. The purpose is to teach the seeker not what to think, but how to think and – far more importantly – how to see that the world is largely an illusion of delusions, created and nurtured by fear, complacency and habit.

Am I saying the world isn't real? Not at all. It is very real, and as paranoid as this might sound, it really is out to get you – not through ninja assassins or shadowy entities looking to steal your soul, but through absorption into the dull and lifeless status quo of so-called normal life.

You will be absorbed if you don't do something. Teachings of the Immortals was designed to provide the seekers for whom it was written with an intense and compelling Awakening. The Darker Teachings are intended to move the traditional reference points from the ordinary to the infinite, from the transient to the eternal.

> *Listen with your heart.*
> *Hear with your spirit.*
> *See with your third eye.*
> *Only then will you Know.*

~

"The Darker Teachings will not only boggle the mind, they have the power to free it – and you – from the yoke of Death itself."
(Night Readers)

"If you read *The Darker Teachings* before you're ready, you may end up holding a candlelight vigil for your sanity. An empowering look at the human potential!"
(Jonathan Abrahms, Independent Reviewer)

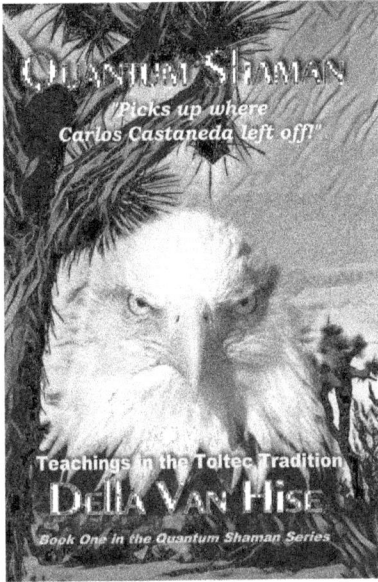

Quantum Shaman: Diary of a Nagual Woman
by Della Van Hise

"Diary of a Nagual Woman brings a quantum understanding to what has traditionally been believed to be a mystical path alone. This book picks up where Carlos Castaneda left off to take us on a roller coaster ride of our own forgotten power..."

When I asked how Orlando had known I would come to this remote location, and how he himself had gotten there – since there were no other cars in the tiny parking lot – he only smiled a little, stretched out his long legs, and slouched down on that cold metal bench to stare up at the stars.

"You're predictable," he said as if I should have already known. "I'm here because this is where you come when you're mad at the world."

I attempted to engage him in a conversation of just exactly how he knew I was mad at the world, since I'd had no direct contact with him in quite some time, nothing to give him any hint of what was going on in my everyday life. But even as I began spelling all of that out to him, he brushed my words aside with an easy gesture.

"Do you want to talk or do you want to waste time looking for logical explanations for every magical thing that ever happens?" he asked. "That's what's wrong with the world, you know. Instead of embracing the mysteries and trying to determine how they might open a crack in an otherwise humdrum, pre-programmed existence, people waste their entire lives explaining it all away, attaching labels to it, filing and categorizing it until it loses any meaning."

He had a point. And I'd already been inundated with enough mysteries to know that some things simply had no explanation humans could understand. *'Magic is only science not yet understood'.* Words Orlando had written more than a year before rattled through my mind up there in the middle of the night, in the middle of nowhere, looking down on a distant world that seemed far more unreal to me at that moment than the world he had been trying to teach me to *see*.

He was there – whether physically or in some spirit-form is ultimately of no importance, for in the sorcerer's world there is no difference between body and spirit, and in any world, perception is reality.

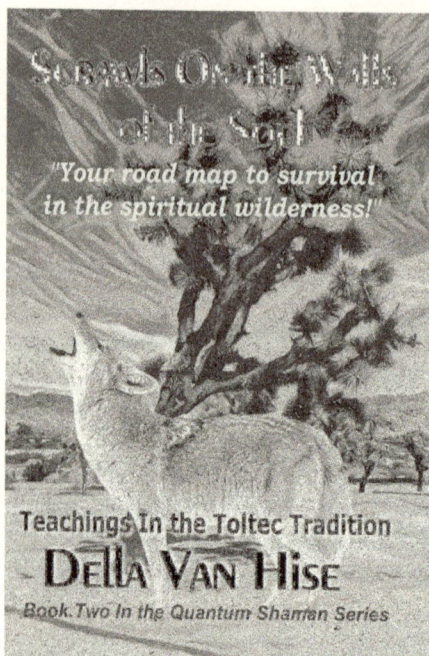

Scrawls on the Walls of the Soul
by Della Van Hise

"If you've ever felt like a stranger in a strange land, this book is your road map to survival in the spiritual wilderness!" (Michael Grove)

The long-awaited follow-up to *Quantum Shaman: Diary of a Nagual Woman*. Stands alone, or order together!

~

It was May of 2000 when my mentor threw me out of the quantum cosmic classroom and said, "I've taught you everything I can. Now it's time to take that knowledge and slam it up against the walls of the real world. If it remains intact and survives the brutality to which it will be subjected, you will get a gold star next to your name and be allowed to proceed to the next level." No mention was made of what this next level might be, or if, indeed, it truly existed.

Go ahead – try to explain this all-consuming path to your friends and relatives. They will smile politely, squirm uncomfortably, and eventually they will stop returning your phone calls and look the other way when they see you coming. And who can blame them? They live in the real world with their office jobs and nuclear families and a host of mindless sitcoms waiting on the propaganda box at the end of their busy day. In direct contrast, it could be observed that anyone who has dedicated themselves to the pursuit of forbidden knowledge really doesn't live in that world at all. Not for lack of wanting, perhaps, but because the real world is quickly seen to be little more than a series of programs and illusions – not unlike The Matrix. And not surprisingly, the people who populate that world may begin to take on a peculiar zombie-like quality. You find yourself alone in a world of jesters, jokers and jackasses. Now what?

~

Available on Amazon in digital or paperback.

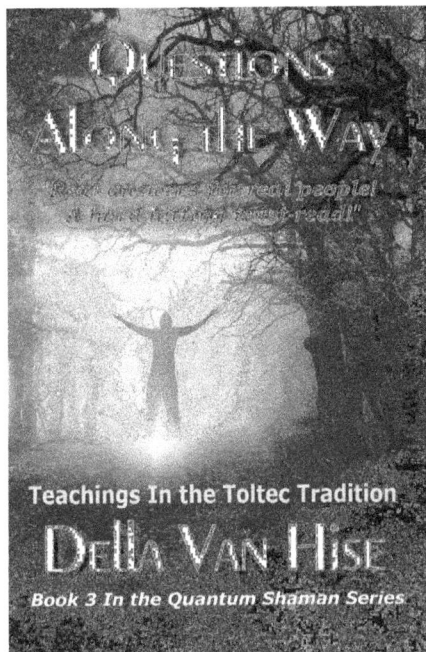

Questions Along the Way
by **Della Van Hise**

Anyone on a journey of personal growth and enlightenment is sure to come face to face with difficult questions that will keep them awake at night and may even plunge them into the dark night of the soul.

In *Questions Along the Way*, Quantum Shaman™ Della Van Hise talks frankly with seekers on the path of heart and opens wide the door to a new understanding that lies beyond the false belief systems and cultural programming all of us must confront when emerging from the dark into the light.

Who am I?
Where am I going?
Is there a God?
Are our lives predestined?
Why am I here?
Who *am* I?

The first and the last question are always the same. And somewhere in between lies the proving ground which we refer to with a simple 4-letter word known as 'Life.' Perhaps for many people these gnawing and persistent questions are nothing more than passing dalliances. But to anyone on a serious path of spiritual evolution and personal growth, these questions form the basis for "the path with heart" – a term used by anthropologist Carlos Castaneda to describe the process of going from an ordinary human being to becoming a man or woman of Knowledge.

INTO THE INFINITE: Opening the Door to the Unknown
by Della Van Hise

Into the Infinite is a compilation of the author's many encounters with the unknown, beginning in early childhood and continuing throughout her adult life. – experiences which compel us to realize the world is nothing like we have been taught to believe.

What can you think when you return from work to find the house cleaned top to bottom... while no one was home?

What do you believe when Carlos Castaneda comes to you in a dream and brings a witch to stop your heart?

What does it mean when you wake at 3:38 a.m. and experience a significant period of missing time between one room and the next?

A truly mind-bending book for anyone who has a love affair with the unknown... or anyone who wants to.

On Amazon in digital & paperback

Scrap of paper torn from the immortal's diary...

~

**I am still only a toddler
in the playpen of eternity.**

www.ingramcontent.com/pod-product-compliance
Lightning Source LLC
Chambersburg PA
CBHW021502090426
42739CB00007B/424